Does It Matter That I'm Saved?

What the Bible Teaches about Salvation

Millard J. Erickson

Study Guides and Teaching Suggestions by Virginia Erickson

D1248628

)ks
.ouse Co
~~p~~ids, Michigan 49516

To my sister,
Eileen Anderson

Published by Baker Books
a division of Baker Book House Company
P.O. Box 6287, Grand Rapids, MI 49516-6287

Printed in the United States of America

Library of Congress Cataloging-in-Publication Data
Erickson, Millard J.
    Does it matter that I'm saved? : what the Bible teaches about salvation / Millard J. Erickson.
       p.   cm.
    Includes bibliographical references.
    ISBN 0-8010-5561-X (pbk.)
    1. Grace (Theology)—Biblical teaching.   2. Salvation—Biblical teaching.   3. Christian life—Biblical teaching. I. Title.
BS680.G7E75   1996
234—dc20
                                      96-1103

Unless otherwise indicated, Scripture quotations are from the New American Standard Bible, © the Lockman Foundation 1960, 1962, 1963, 1971, 1973, 1975, 1977. Other versions cited include the King James Version (KJV) and the Revised Standard Version (RSV).

Contents

Preface

Fads in the Christian life come and go, but the basic truths of what it means to be a Christian do not change. Our understanding of what happens when a person accepts Jesus Christ and what God continues to do in the life of the believer affects our ability to cooperate with this divine working, and contributes to our enjoyment of that experience. This book is an attempt to help believers appreciate more fully and grow in that salvation that God desires everyone to have. In the years since this little volume first appeared, some Christians have tended to neglect the richness of the biblical teaching regarding salvation, thus losing something of the full-orbed Christian experience. If the renewing of our minds is part of salvation, then the study of these important doctrines is part of God's intention for us as new creatures.

I wish to thank Jim Weaver and the editorial staff of Baker Books for reissuing this book. I also wish to thank the administration of Victor Books, the original publishers, for granting permission to bring out this new edition. I have especially appreciated the opportunity of working with my wife, Ginny, in a new role, as she wrote the study guides and teacher's helps for this book. We have been able to share together the struggles and joys of authorship. Her work greatly enhances the book's usefulness for lay persons. Several lay members of Central Community Church of Minneapolis, a multiracial, multiethnic congregation, assisted me in evaluating possible titles for the book.

May this book be used by the Spirit of God to build up believers in faith, hope, and love, and in the likeness of Jesus Christ.

1

Who Am I?

Brakes screech. The sound of skidding tires follows; then, a dull thud. A human body, struck by a rapidly moving automobile, is thrown against a parked car and then crumples limply to the pavement. Quickly a crowd gathers, including a police officer. An ambulance is called, but it is apparent that the man is already dead. The policeman searches the body for identification, but finds none. "Does anyone know who this man is?" he inquires. No one knows him.

Who am I? Where did I come from? Where am I going? These are questions that sooner or later press in on all human beings. Humans can ignore everything around them, but they cannot escape the fact of themselves.

Attempts to Identify Humanity

A number of sources seem to have the answers to these questions. Biology tells us about our physical makeup, how our bodies work, what goes wrong with them, how they are to be made well. Intense research is going on continuously in these areas, telling us ever more about ourselves. Psychology is discovering more about the mental and emotional nature of the human race and about each individual person. Sociology tells us how humans function in groups, while cultural anthropology informs us about people in various cultures. Anthropology also seeks to reach back into the dim past of the human race's beginnings and development. Interest in genealogy has received new impetus, as the *Roots* phenomenon spreads. More and more of us want to find out who we are in terms of our ancestors.

With all this information, we ought to know ourselves better than ever. More basic questions, however, still press upon us. Where did I really come from, not merely in terms of a generation or two back in my past, but what is the ultimate source of my being? Do I exist simply as a result of a combination of accidental occurrences? Or is life a gift from some Higher Being who created me? If so, what is his purpose for humanity, in bringing us into being?

The possibility that we have been created by God raises other questions as well. What does he expect of us? What is necessary to please him, or to be properly related to him? What is my present relationship to him? What should I do to make it better? What is God trying to do in my life? What has he promised to do? And what does the future hold?

Salvation and the "Big Picture" of Theology

This type of questioning leads us to the doctrine of salvation. But before we can understand the various aspects of this complex teaching, we must look closely at other areas of Christian doctrine.

Christian theology is organic. It is not a collection of

separate, unconnected topics. Rather, teaching in one area vitally affects teaching in another area. So, for example, our understanding of the nature of God influences our concept of the human condition. If God were only love, if he were benevolent and indulgent, then our problem would not be so serious. If this were so, God could just overlook our shortcomings. There would be no real need to appease him. On the other hand, if God is perfectly holy and righteous and cannot accept imperfection or weakness, then our problem is much more serious. If we do anything less than completely fulfill God's will, we are alienated from God.

To put it another way, salvation is a relational matter. Its concepts are not independent ones, like *three* or *red*. They are relational concepts like *left of*, *after*, or *behind*, concepts that cannot stand by themselves. Something cannot simply be to the left of, or after, or behind. It must be to the left of, after, or behind something else. Even in cases where the statement seems to make sense alone, a close examination will generally reveal that a point of reference is assumed.

The Human Problem

The Bible states that humans were created by God. As the last and highest of the earth creatures, the man and the woman alone were made in God's image (Gen. 1:26–27). God intended them to have communion with him, to converse and interact with him (Gen. 1:28–30; 2:16–17). They were also given dominion over the rest of creation, to supervise it and develop it to its intended potential (Gen. 1:28).

But they were expected to obey God. Disobedience to God proved to be their downfall. They were allowed to eat of the fruit of every tree of the Garden of Eden except one: the tree of the knowledge of good and evil (Gen. 2:17). As a result of temptation by the serpent, Eve was deceived and sinned. Then she encouraged Adam to do the same (Gen. 3:1–17). He did, and they came under God's curse for their disobedience. They *deserved* God's punishment for that sin: death (Rom. 6:23).

What Adam and Eve did, all of us have repeated in our own lives (Rom. 3:23). If we think it was unfortunate that Adam sinned, we must realize that, given the same situation, all of us would do exactly the same thing. In fact, that is just what we are continually proving by our own sins.

The sin of Adam, however, did not affect Adam alone. Some theologians say that each person begins life just as Adam and Eve did—innocent, untainted, and perfectly capable of choosing to do good. But Paul clearly refutes this idea in Romans 5. Sin was not one individual's isolated act. It involves the entire human race: "Therefore, just as through one man sin entered into the world, and death through sin, and so death spread to all men, because all sinned" (v. 12). There are numerous explanations of just how this takes place, but the effect is the same, regardless. All sinned, all are sinners, and all receive the consequences of sin—death. So apparently all are also guilty.

We do not merely sin; *we are sinners.* Our very nature is inclined toward sin. Whereas before the fall Adam and Eve were at least as able to abstain from sin as to commit it, now we all tend naturally to sin. There is a "drag" on our desire and ability to do God's will. It appears that something in our very nature has been "spoiled" by sin.

Guilt is another problem. Not only has death come upon human bodies through *original* sin, but as each person continues to violate God's will, so he or she incurs God's wrath and punishment. Thus, we continually separate ourselves from God's presence and favor. Restitution must somehow be made, so that there can be forgiveness and acceptance.

One more thing remains, however. Humans are not only sinners, guilty in the sight of the Law and the Judge. They have also lost that friendship and love relationship they originally had with God. Sin is like a quarrel between a parent and a child. God's aim was not merely to remove his children from their condition as criminals. He wanted the warmth and closeness of fellowship to be restored. He intended more than pardon. What he wanted was reconciliation, a restoration of the parent–child relationship.

God gave Adam and Eve a choice: They could obey or disobey. If they obeyed, there would be reward; if they disobeyed, there would be punishment. God could have said: "They had their chance and they failed! That is their problem now. I am washing my hands of the whole matter." God was free to say this and to abandon the human race. He owed us nothing more. In fact, he owed humans nothing in the beginning. He could have simply considered the creation of the human race an unsuccessful experiment.

The nature of God, however, would not permit him to do this. He still loved humans, and he wanted to regain the relationship that he had originally intended. Although under no obligation to do so, he would give them another chance. But how? That was the crucial issue.

God's Solution

One possible solution might be for God to wipe the slate clean. He would simply, out of the compassion of his heart, cancel humans' sin and treat them as if nothing had ever happened. He would overlook sin. This would be pure forgiveness. Certainly, if human beings can do this with one another, God can do it too. He should not be less forgiving and generous than the best of human beings, should he? Why should a loving God insist on demanding punishment for sin? If he does not really want to condemn humans, why should he?

As ideal as this solution might seem, it was not in keeping with God's nature. God is holy. For him to allow persons in that sinful state to enter his presence, to have fellowship with him, would require a compromise of his own holy nature. It would be a denial of what he is. Just as God cannot sin, so he cannot ignore sin. The Bible makes clear that this was neither God's solution nor one of his options. We should not think of this inability to excuse sin as some weakness on God's part. It is rather a tribute to the greatness of his purity and holiness. The idea of a God who overlooks sin may seem attractive, but it contradicts the fatherhood of God. It pictures him as an indulgent, permissive grandfather whose actions would not, in the long run, really benefit the other party.

The second solution would be for the individual to alter his or her own behavior to become pleasing to God. This requires offering some payment to compensate for the wrong done and providing a positive goodness. But this creates another problem. Humans, at best, can only fulfill what is currently required of them. Even if they lived a life of perfect obedience from this point forward, they would only be doing what is expected. They would have nothing additional to balance out their previous wrongdoing. Death is the penalty required for sin. And humans are still liable for their sins.

In addition, no one is capable of living perfectly from this point on. Paul's expression is instructive here: "I am not practicing what I would like to do, but I am doing the very thing I hate" (Rom. 7:15). Thus, the problem of human guilt (or sinful state) and the problem of sinful nature or tendency make these two possible solutions untenable.

One alternative remains. If God must require the payment of sin's penalty, and if humans are unable to fulfill the Law's demands, then to keep them from damnation someone else must assume and fulfill those demands. But who?

It must be someone who could offer God something for which he or she is not obligated. Ideally, this would be a perfect person who has no personal liability and thus is able to do something additional on behalf of someone else. In effect God solved the problem by retaining the requirement of the Law, but fulfilling it himself. God came into our world as Jesus of Nazareth; he became a human, without ceasing to be God.

As the God-man, Jesus was subject to all the normal conditions of human existence, with the exception of sin. He lived a perfect life and fulfilled the Law perfectly. He met all of God's requirements, for he was genuinely tempted, yet did not sin at any point. Because he did not sin, he was not under the judgment of death. But by dying, he could offer something to God that he was not obligated to give, and thus provide atonement for human sin. This he did and the Father accepted it as equivalent to the death of all humankind.

Now human beings potentially have the status of being righteous with God. But this righteousness accomplished by Christ doesn't fulfill its purpose unless it is accepted. As a gift, it is free, but it is never forced upon anyone. It is necessary for each individual to turn from his or her wicked, independent ways and to respond to God's initiative.

As we differentiate the aspects of the doctrine of salvation, we may designate this initial step as *conversion*, which means literally "a turning." It involves two elements: a repudiation of sin, termed *repentance,* and a trust in and acceptance of Christ, called *faith.*

Conversion is a human's response to God's working in his or her life. When converted, one begins a new relationship with God. God credits him or her with the righteousness that Christ provided by his death and resurrection. God declares the believer to be what he now perceives him or her to be: righteous. We call this judicial act of God *justification.* It is possible because of the believer's union with Christ. Christ has assumed the sinner's debt and the new believer is a joint possessor of Christ's righteousness. This is not an infusion of righteousness, but rather a declarative action.

God not only pardons us, but he welcomes us back as children. This is *adoption.* We are restored to all the benefits of membership in God's family, including the Father's love and favor. We are no longer strangers and aliens. We become his offspring, in a vital sense.

A further problem needs to be examined. Unless one's basic nature changes, that person will continue to violate God's will. So God alters the nature of each one who trusts in him. He places a new nature within, canceling the effect of the fall and actually imparting a new quality to the person's life. The Bible speaks of this radical change as a new birth, or *regeneration.*

Yet this new birth is only that—a birth or beginning. God continues to work in the believer's life, developing the spiritual dimension that he originally planned for humankind to have. This growth in holiness means that the Christian actually becomes what his or her status already is. The Bible calls this *sanctification.*

As God works in the believer's life he also provides for the fears and dangers there. He gives *assurance* of salvation to Christians lest they doubt that they have really been saved. Similarly, he gives believers the grace of *perseverance* in the faith, lest they abandon their love and commitment to him and fall away. God provides positive means to these ends.

This process of growth and development does not come to complete fulfillment within this life, but we are promised that one day it will be completely fulfilled. We shall be like Jesus and shall share in his glory. This is *glorification.*

Thus, God's gift becomes the solution to that apparent dilemma we observed earlier. What God requires, he also provides. He does not compromise his holiness or his love. The two coincide in the gift of salvation. It is God's doing, not ours. It is an obtainment, not an attainment. We must respond to God's working and cooperate with it at a number of points, but even in this, God is at work motivating and enabling us in the process. In the final analysis, salvation becomes of value to us when we accept it as God's free gift.

After distinguishing these aspects of salvation, we should note that they are only logical distinctions, or ways of viewing one great truth. They are not a series of separate actions on God's part. Neither are they a series of separate events. Several of these elements occur simultaneously. While it is helpful to think of certain of these aspects of our salvation as depending on another one already having taken place, the order is *only* logical, not an order-of-time sequence.

Some may be hesitant to examine something as wonderful as salvation, lest in the process some of the wonder of it should be lost. This need not be true. Yet it need not disturb us. Our appreciation for what God has done should grow rather than diminish as we come to understand it fully, and our devotion, love, and gratitude should increase.

We might draw a parallel to the study of human anatomy. As our understanding of the functioning of the different bones and muscles grows, we might be less impressed with the body, thinking, "Oh, I know how all of that operates. It is merely a matter of certain principles of physics and chemistry." That might be the case, but more often it is not. The more fully a person comes to understand the human organism, the greater is his or her sense of awe.

Another danger is to become so preoccupied with the explanation of salvation that we fail to experience it. This is like the centipede who walked very well until one day someone admired him, and asked him how he maneuvered all of those limbs with such perfect timing. As the centipede thought about it, he saw the complexity of his coordination, and became immobilized. We must make certain that our added understanding of salvation is accompanied by spiritual growth.

The term "born again" is used quite widely in our society, and is even applied outside of a religious context. In 1976 the Gallup Poll revealed that one-third of all American adults thought of themselves as "born again," and the American electorate elected a president who unashamedly described himself as "born again." In light of this, *Newsweek* magazine proclaimed 1976 the "Year of the Evangelical." More recent polls show a similarly large percentage of the population who identify themselves as "born again." What does this really mean? In this book we will be examining this vital evangelical core of the Christian faith.

Salvation and Societal Sin

Sin not only has an individual effect; it also has a societal dimension. Thus, the collective force of evil takes on proportions much greater than the sum of its individual parts. Today's society is filled with many evils. Unfair distribution of power, unjust practices, forces of competition, discrimination, hatred, crime, and even war contribute to the evil of individuals. These factors place temptation in the way of people, inducing them to sin. Certainly such situations are not pleasing to God and need to be changed.

In light of this, some Christians believe that we obtain salvation by concerning ourselves with the group rather than with the individual. We must modify the structures of society, they say, and when we do, individual evil will also disappear.

Various philosophies state this in different ways. Dialectical materialism, better known as Marxism, holds that the human problem is ultimately material or economic in nature. A classless society, in which no private individual owns any means of production, will see all evil simply wither away. Certain revolutionary groups in this country and elsewhere feel that the problem lies in our present society, which must be completely torn down. When that is done, humans will be free in their natural state and will be good. Others feel that adequate education for all will remove the difficulties. Yet others believe that laws guaranteeing equal status and rights for all in a society will eliminate evil.

All of these views correctly note the influence environment exerts on individual behavior. To be sure, some problems in society must be directly attacked in order to alleviate them. The Bible, however, teaches that individual humans are not basically good. Society will only be changed from the inside out. As individuals are born again by the grace of God and then unitedly seek to change the evil in the world, society will change. As difficult as the transformation of human personalities may seem, Jesus had in mind the ability to change lives when he said, "All things are possible with God" (Mark 10:27).

Study Guide

Key Questions

1. Explain what the author means when he says, "Christianity is organic. It is not a collection of separate, unconnected topics."
2. Why is it fair that humanity can be condemned because of Adam and Eve's sin?
3. What are two essential elements of conversion to Christianity?
4. Briefly explain the following terms as the author describes them: justification, adoption, regeneration, sanctification, glorification.

Personal Application

1. Regeneration and new birth are interchangeable terms. Can you list some similarities between physical birth and spiritual birth? Why is calling regeneration "new birth" such a powerful metaphor?
2. What God requires (payment of sin's penalty), he also provides (Jesus' death for our sin). Can you think of ways this same truth might also be applied to growth, temptation, and sin in a Christian's life?

For Further Thought

1. If *Newsweek* called 1976 the "year of the evangelical," what do you think the magazine might say about evangelicalism in this present year? Why?
2. How should Christians approach the problems of evil in our society, since we know that the way to permanent change is through personal spiritual regeneration? How many ways can we address these multifaceted problems?

2

An About-Face

Today conversion is newsworthy. Charles Colson, one of the central figures in the Watergate scandal, in the midst of his inner struggle turned to faith in Jesus Christ. Renouncing his old way of life, he adopted new values and objectives, amazing those who had known him best. Stories like his are repeated over and over, with well-known persons as well as those with less public visibility. If not a household term, conversion is at least a familiar expression. Some cynics question that reality which the word represents. Others loudly acclaim the dramatic impact of Christian conversion. But the phenomenon, however we evaluate it, is unquestionably with us.

The Meaning of Conversion

In its most basic sense, the word *conversion* denotes a turning, a change of direction and allegiance. In noun form it appears only once in the Bible: "They were passing through both Phoenicia and Samaria, describing in detail the conversion of the Gentiles" (Acts 15:3). The verb form, however, appears numerous times in both the Old and New Testaments. It is often rendered "turn," "turn again," or "return." The meaning can be clearly seen in the purely literal instances, such as, "If it (the house) is not worthy, let your greeting of peace *return* to you" (Matt. 10:13); "and let him who is in the field not *turn back* to get his cloak" (Matt. 24:18); "Let us *return* and visit the brethren in every city in which we proclaimed the word of the Lord, and see how they are" (Acts 15:36).

In the spiritual application of the concept, conversion denotes a similarly clear change in direction of life. A mass conversion is described in Acts 9:35: "And all who lived at Lydda and Sharon saw him, and they *turned* to the Lord." Paul's conversion included a commission "to open their eyes so that they may *turn* from darkness to light and from the dominion of Satan to God" (Acts 26:18). This indicates a shifting of a person's most fundamental loyalties. The concept may be used to describe turning from the right way to the wrong way, as in Galatians 4:9: "But now that you have come to know God, or rather to be known by God, how is it that you *turn back* again to the weak and worthless elemental things, to which you desire to be enslaved all over again?" Most frequently, however, it describes turning from the wrong way to the right way.

Conversion as Return

In many of the New Testament usages, the idea of returning, of reassuming the former relationship or at least the one intended, is implied. The prodigal son is a classic expression of this (Luke 15:11–32). He was going back home, returning to his father, who was still his father in spite of all of the son's rebellion. There is a sort of rightness about conversion to God and Christ.

The Bible teaches that humans alone, of all God's creatures, were created in the image of God (Gen. 1:26–27). Theologians have long debated just what that means, but virtually all agree that the image of God enables human beings to be related to God. Although sin entered the human race and affected that image, it was not totally obliterated. Fallen humanity is still described as "in the image of God" (Gen. 9:6). Our purpose and destiny is still to know God and to have a relationship with him. Life apart from God is incomplete, less than God intended. Consequently, it tends to be dissatisfying and frustrating.

This was Augustine's experience. Reared in the Catholic faith by a mother who continued to pray for him, he sought satisfaction from many different sources. He plunged into a life of reckless immorality but found it unsatisfying. Then he pursued more intellectual courses of action, seeking gratification in the philosophy of Manichaeism. Finally, after entertaining the philosophy of Neoplatonism, he came to Christ. Sitting in a garden one day he heard the voice of a child in the next garden, saying repeatedly, "Take and read." He turned and saw a Bible on a table near him. He opened it to Romans 13:14: "But put on the Lord Jesus Christ, and make no provision for the flesh." Augustine turned to Christ, and found the end of his search. He later wrote: "We are made for thee, O God, and our hearts are restless until they find rest in thee." If Augustine is right, there is an incompleteness to the life of the non-Christian. While not always correctly identified, it is nonetheless there.

Saul of Tarsus was encountered by the Lord on the Damascus road. God stopped him in his tracks with a blinding light. A voice from heaven said, "Saul, Saul, why are you persecuting Me? It is hard for you to kick against the goads" (Acts 26:14). The goads were sharp objects used to direct an ox where the master wanted him to go. Resistance to the direction of the master's will was painful. Similarly, it was difficult and even painful for Paul to attempt to live contrary to God's plan. Hence, the Christians who were accused of "turning the world upside down" (Acts 17:6) were not really doing so. More correctly, they were turning it right side up by bringing people into a right relationship to God.

Conversion, then, is clearly a change. It must be this, for the natural human direction is away from a total commitment to God. Some believe that all we need is a slight modification of the thrust of our lives, or a supplementing of tendencies that are otherwise basically correct. This idea is emphatically contrary to the biblical doctrine of conversion and its necessity. A radical reversal is essential. Conversion has a negative aspect (repentance) and a positive aspect (faith). In this chapter we will consider the characteristics of conversion in general, leaving the specific examination of faith and repentance to later chapters.

Barriers to Conversion

One barrier to conversion is indifference or apathy. Many people are unsaved not because they have deliberately rejected the person of Jesus Christ, but because they have never seriously considered Christ as the Redeemer. Preoccupied with other matters, they never take seriously the issues of life, and so they fail to consider Christianity. These are people for whom "Christ is the answer" makes no real sense; they are unaware of their spiritual needs. For such persons, the major change involved in conversion consists primarily in awakening to the issue, seeing the need.

Blaise Pascal faced such indifference as he considered the attitudes of seventeenth-century Frenchmen. They did not reject Christianity; they merely bypassed it. To arrest the attention of these aloof Frenchmen, Pascal developed and propounded his famous wager: Consider the question of whether there is a God. Suppose you wager that God is. If you are right, you have gained everything. If you are wrong, you have lost nothing. Should you wager, however, that God is not and he is, you have lost all.

Pascal's aim was to alert people to the seriousness of the choice, in view of the infinite stakes involved. To decline to wager is in effect to wager that God is not. Jesus spoke to the same issue when he said, "For what will a man be profited, if he gains the whole world, and forfeits his soul? Or what will a man give in exchange for his soul?" (Matt. 16:26). He was emphasizing the crucial importance of carefully investigating and consciously choosing, for what is at stake is one's soul, one's self, one's whole life. Conversion, then, may make its fundamental reversal at the level of attitude, from indifference and neglect to concerned investigation and evaluation.

A second barrier to conversion is unbelief. This involves persons who are concerned and have probably inquired about Christianity's truthfulness. But they either believe Christianity to be false or are at least uncertain about its truth claims. For such people, conversion calls for persuasion and conviction. In some cases, such as Nicodemus, there may be openness to the truth but an inability to comprehend it. In some cases, conversion may well come through a process of reasoning. C. S. Lewis's conversion was of this type. An openness to the possibility of Christianity's truth is a minimum prerequisite for the conversion of such persons. Sincere, conscientious persons like this, genuinely desiring to know the truth so that they can follow it, move quickly to faith once intellectual conviction occurs.

A third hindrance is conflict, or divided loyalty. Some people have an attachment to a person or possession that they are unwilling to give up. They feel that becoming a Christian, with the subsequent necessity of altering their way of life, is a sacrifice too great to make. They are not willing to surrender the thing that gives meaning to their lives. The prodigal son is an example. He had to realize that he was not finding what he really wanted in life before he determined to return home. Many people fall into this category. For them, conversion is not usually the result of an intellectual persuasion. They need to live longer, until they experience the emptiness, the inadequacy, the ultimately unsatisfying nature of their lives. Conversion for such people may come as a result of boredom, or of finally arriving at a point of disgust with their own lives.

Another barrier to conversion is a sense of unworthiness. Some persons believe that they are just too wicked to be saved. They may even think themselves unworthy of approaching the Lord. This low self-image is countered when they realize that the Lord really is a gracious God who offers salvation as a genuine gift.

The opposite problem is a lack of the sense of sin. Some persons consider themselves too good to need Christ. Usually genuinely moral people, they are attempting to be good enough to please God on their own. Certainly Saul of Tarsus was like this. In later life he described the conscientiousness with which he endeavored to fulfill every point of righteousness (Phil. 3:4–6). For such persons the real difficulty lies in admitting their own inadequacy and need. Usually this comes when they recognize the discrepancy between the ideal of what they want to be and what they actually are. Pride has to be overcome if these persons are to accept the offer of salvation. Like the "unworthy" person, the difficulty here is acknowledging the idea of salvation by grace. This person has trouble admitting the necessity of salvation by grace, whereas the other individual is almost afraid to believe in the possibility of such grace.

A final obstacle is self-sufficiency. This is found in persons who feel no need of Christ, because they can solve all the problems of their lives themselves. Like the person lacking a sense of sin, they may not have a keen moral sense. They are generally capable and resourceful persons, whose occupation may involve solving problems by their own efforts and shrewdness. They see no need of God in their lives. They are perfectly able to deal with their problems. Frequently, there is no conversion for such persons until a real crisis comes that they cannot handle—a serious illness, the loss of a loved one, the breakup of a marriage, the collapse of a career.

A genuine transformation is needed even in these moral and pious people because God requires complete commitment. "You shall love the Lord your God with all your heart, and with all your soul, and with all your strength, and with all your mind" (Luke 10:27). The Lord must be first. Among those who would follow Christ, nothing must interfere. "No one can serve two masters," said Jesus, "for either he will hate the one and love the other, or he will hold to one and despise the other. You cannot serve God and Mammon" (an Aramaic word for wealth or possessions; Matt. 6:24).

The Lord's demand for complete commitment is demonstrated in the story of one young man who came to Jesus wanting to know how to inherit eternal life. He had kept all the laws his entire life. If there was yet another law that he should keep, he wanted to know about it, so he could do it. Jesus, however, struck at the one point of his reservation, telling him to sell every-thing, give all the proceeds to the poor, and then to come and follow him. At this demand, the young man went away sorrowful, for he had great wealth (Matt. 19:16–22).

A similar instance appears in the life of Abraham, who was called to offer his most prized possession, his son Isaac, to Jehovah as a sacrifice. God tested the patriarch's priorities. It was a specific example of the word given by Jesus: "He who loves father or mother more than Me is not worthy of Me" (Matt. 10:37).

In neither of these cases would the sacrifice ever have actually been required. Indeed, in the case of Abraham, we know that it was not. It was a test of whether Abraham wholeheartedly trusted God, or whether he was holding something back.

The first of the Ten Commandments contains the same concept: "You shall have no other gods before Me" (Exod. 20:3). The problem with the Israelites was not that they were abandoning worship of Jehovah to pursue other gods. Nor were they even inclined to put worship of these other gods ahead of Jehovah. Rather, they were dividing their religious commitment between Jehovah and the idols. The Lord *alone* must be worshiped, for he alone is the only true and living God. Whenever we have other objects of worship—idols, whether tangible or intangible—we are in need of conversion. Otherwise, we are like the double-minded man of whom James writes (James 1:7–8), unstable and ineffectual.

Types of Conversion Experience

The word "conversion" means different things to different people. Sometimes conversion occurs in a dramatic way, with a cataclysmic reversal of direction in life. This was the case with Saul, when he was converted and became the Apostle Paul. The Lord appeared to him in a miraculous revelation that left him temporarily blind. The reversal of his life was sharp and unmistakable. From a determined and zealous opponent of the followers of Christ (Acts 9:1–2), he became an equally energetic advocate of Christ (Acts 9:22). There was never a doubt in Paul's mind regarding the change that had taken place, or when and where it had occurred. The reversal was so sharp, however, that some believers doubted its genuineness (Acts 9:13–14).

Not all conversions, however, take place under such circumstances. Just a few chapters later in the Book of Acts (16:11–15), we find the account of a woman named Lydia who became a believer. She was evidently one of those "God-fearers" who would gather to listen at Jewish worship services. She responded to Paul's message. But we find few details of her conversion. "The Lord opened her heart to respond to the things spoken by Paul" (Acts 16:14). What a beautiful picture! Calmly and quietly, the Lord opened her heart so that she responded. Lydia had first accepted the message and practices of Judaism; now, upon hearing the gospel of Jesus Christ, she made the easy transition to the Christian way. No sharp and dramatic break was necessary.

All this suggests that we need to distinguish conversion from the circumstances of conversion. Conversion is simply a turning. As such, it may take place suddenly and sharply, or gradually and less dramatically. The essential point is that conversion does not simply happen naturally, as an uninterrupted development or progression.

At times we may be in danger of giving the impression that the climactic turn is the desired and normal experience. Perhaps this has been reinforced by a type of evangelistic preaching modeled after frontier revivalism. Life on the frontier was tenuous and the visits of the preacher relatively infrequent. Consequently, the preaching of the gospel took on a special note of urgency. Preaching aimed at a strong sense of sin and the necessity of an immediate decision. Frequently the preacher applied a considerable amount of emotional pressure in giving the "invitation." "Night-to-day" conversions became the pattern.

This, however, is not the only genuine kind of conversion. The Lydia type of experience is equally valid. Many factors determine the type of experience that accompanies a conversion. An individual's personality, previous experience, and the particular way God chooses to work in a given case make a great deal of difference. For example, a person who has engaged in gross sin—immorality and perhaps even crime—is more likely to experience a sharp break with the past than a person who has lived a comparatively respectable life. Similarly, an individual who over a prolonged period of time has been exposed to the facts of the gospel is more likely to have a gradual, quiet conversion, than a person to whom the Christian message comes as a revelation of something totally new.

The circumstances of the conversion experience are not the measure of the validity of that conversion. In popular evangelical circles, we have at times elevated the dramatic conversion as a sort of proof of the truth of the gospel. Psychology has often directed its attention to this type of experience and it has frequently drawn close parallels to nonreligious conversions, such as conversions to communism. Such study, however, does not undermine the supernatural character of Christian conversion. The fact is that any change of allegiance can be a dramatic emotional happening—even a turning to a godless philosophy such as communism. The quiet turning to God of a Lydia is as supernatural as the dramatic conversion of a Saul. Those who have had a spectacular conversion experience should not take any special pride in it; neither should those who lack this type of experience feel inferior.

Conversion and Conversions

Logically there is one conversion: at the beginning of the Christian life. Note, however, that there may also be other, later turnings. A person who strays from God needs to turn back to him. Thus, Jesus said that although Peter would deny him, Peter would "turn again," or experience another conversion subsequent to his first or major conversion (Luke 22:32). We might say that there is one Conversion, but possibly many conversions.

Study Guide

Key Questions

1. How do Paul's experience of salvation and his life before and after bear out the statement that life apart from God is dissatisfying (Acts 9:1–31; chaps. 13–28)?
2. What are two general characteristics of conversion, according to the author?
3. List five barriers people face today. Which do you think is the most prevalent among your acquaintances? Are all equally hard to deal with in our evangelization efforts?

Bible Investigation

1. Find examples of the author's five barriers to conversion in Bible characters, both Old Testament and New Testament. List as many as you can.
2. Relate this chapter to the story of the rich young ruler (Matt. 19:16–23).

3. How do Jesus' words about becoming as little children before entering the kingdom of heaven relate to salvation (Matt. 18:2–6)?

Personal Application

1. If there are barriers that keep people from accepting salvation, are there also barriers that keep people from becoming mature Christians? Are they similar kinds of barriers? Are there additional ones?
2. In view of the author's list of barriers to salvation, how might we best prepare ourselves to witness to our friends?

For Further Thought

1. The author lists five barriers to conversion. Can you think of any others from your experience? Do some of the barriers overlap? Are there some barriers that might be more prevalent for young college students? incarcerated prisoners? young people? older people?
2. In regard to Pascal's wager, it seems like such an easy decision to accept salvation. How does this relate to the so-called deathbed conversions we hear about? Can deathbed conversions be genuine? Why or why not?

3

I'm Truly Sorry

The most difficult words in the English language to say are not the longest words or some complicated scientific terms. The most difficult words to utter are "I was wrong" and "I am sorry." But these words are the very heart of repentance.

Repentance and faith, which together constitute conversion, are scarcely separable. They are two different ways of looking at the same thing, or two different perspectives on the same process. They are mutually interdependent. We only have faith in the true sense because we are repentant. We repent because we have faith.

The Basic Meaning of Repentance

In its most basic sense, repentance means "turning away" from one's sins. It is drawn from two different words in the Hebrew Old Testament and a corresponding pair of words in the New Testament. One of these Hebrew words means "to sigh or pant or groan" and is what we call an onomatopoeic word: the very sound of the word resembles a sigh. It expresses the remorse, sorrow, and regret that we often feel when we are conscious of wrong that we have done. It is grief felt over sin or its consequences. In the Old Testament it is most frequently used of God. His grief over sin was not for any sin of his own but for human sins. In the New Testament the word depicts Judas's sense of remorse over his betrayal of Jesus (Matt. 27:3).

Another aspect of repentance is expressed by different words in both the Old and New Testaments. These emphasize a radical change or reversal of attitudes and actions. In the New Testament, it is the basic thrust of John the Baptist's opening message: "Now in those days John the Baptist came, preaching in the wilderness of Judea, saying, 'Repent, for the kingdom of heaven is at hand'" (Matt. 3:1–2). It was also, as we shall note later, a basic part of the message of Jesus and the apostles.

Repentance as Conviction of Sin

Genuine repentance is distinguished by several characteristics. The first is conviction of one's sin. This is the intellectual element: believing that "I am a sinner." Conviction means being convinced of something. The Holy Spirit's work in conviction is convincing persons that they are sinners. Jesus promised that the Spirit would perform this role: "And He, when He comes, will convict the world concerning sin . . . because they do not believe in Me" (John 16:8–9).

It is one thing for me to believe that you are a sinner, or that some other person is a sinner. It is even reasonably easy to conclude that everyone else is a sinner. But to admit to myself and to God that *I* am a sinner is far more difficult.

Actually, the enunciation of the syllables in admitting guilt is simple. *Wrong* is not difficult to say. It is no problem to include it in "He is wrong," and may even bring some satisfaction in connection with "You are wrong." Similarly, *I am* presents no intrinsic difficulty. Those syllables "I am right" roll out smoothly. But to put *I* and *wrong* together is another thing. It is painful. It is costly, for it strikes at my pride. It is bad enough when I am incorrect because of wrong information. This is inaccuracy. But when I have acted wrongly, it is more difficult to admit because it reflects on me as a person. My desire to protect my ego makes it difficult for me to recognize my sin and to see things as they really are.

David is a perfect example. He sinned by desiring and then committing adultery with Bathsheba. To cover his sin, he arranged the death of Bathsheba's husband, Uriah—a scheme equivalent to murder. Somehow David failed to recognize his own sin until God sent Nathan the prophet to confront him with it. Nathan could have come to the king and said, "What do you think of a king who has numerous wives and concubines and is not satisfied, so he takes the only wife of one of his soldiers?" Had Nathan said that, David would have understood Nathan's message, become defensive, and tried to justify himself and his actions.

Instead of a direct approach, Nathan used a parable. He spoke in such a way that David recognized the truth in itself, but did not see that it directly involved him. David reacted to the message *objectively.* He judged it on its own merits first, and then he reacted to the way it affected him personally.

Nathan told a story of a rich man who had many flocks and herds and a poor man who had only one little ewe lamb that was like a daughter to him. When a traveler came to the rich man, instead of taking one of his abundant flock or herd to feed him, he took the poor man's lamb (2 Sam. 12:1–4).

David recognized the injustice of this action. He reacted violently: "As the LORD lives, surely the man who has done this deserves to die. And he must make restitution for the lamb fourfold, because he did this thing and had no compassion" (vv. 5–6). It was only then, when David judged the act in itself, that Nathan identified him as the man (vv. 7–12). At that point David acknowledged his sin (v. 13).

Conviction of sin means more than acknowledging the fact of our sin. It means accepting responsibility for it. Conviction is not just agreement that we have sinned. It is admission that we are sinners.

Here again, the natural wickedness of the human heart must be overcome. We may admit to an act, but decline to label it as sin. Or we may try to rationalize our actions.

In the first case, if we can find some good result from the action, we may call the action "good" because of that effect. David might have described his action with Bathsheba not as adultery but as "bringing companionship and comfort to a lonely woman" in the prolonged absence of her husband.

In the second case, we may note the reactions of the first sinners to their sin. Adam, when confronted with his action, responded by saying, "The woman you put here with me—she gave me some fruit from the tree and I ate it" (Gen. 3:12). Notice how Adam blamed everyone but himself. First he passed the guilt to Eve. "If she had not given me the fruit," Adam seems to be saying, "I would never have sinned." But there is also a partial blaming of God: "The woman *you* put here with me . . ." Here the hint appears to be: "If you hadn't given me the woman, I would not have sinned." Eve quickly followed the same pattern: "The serpent deceived me, and I ate" (v. 13).

So we avoid repentance by denying that we really are at fault. But for certain causes, we say, we would not have done what we did. These explanations of sin in terms of such causal factors as biological necessity, genetic determination, childhood conditioning, or monetary circumstances have the common goal of shifting the responsibility for our actions.

Genuine repentance is quite different. In Psalm 51, David expressed his feelings regarding his sin. He did not speak of "mistakes," "weaknesses," "oversights," or "failures." He did not blame his actions on conditioning or contributing factors. Rather, he spoke of "my transgressions" (v. 1), "my sin" (v. 2), "evil" (v. 4), and "my sins" and "my iniquities" (v. 9), and identified the "bloodguiltiness" (v. 14). Here was a man who recognized the nature of his actions and accepted the responsibility for his sin.

In view of our natural resistance to conviction of sin, we must remember that the Holy Spirit performs this convincing ministry. He uses human efforts to accomplish it. So in dealing with people we should be thorough, persuasive, and tactful. If we attempt to bring conviction by our ability alone, we will encounter resistance. We might receive (literally) a black eye for our efforts. And, more important, such an approach will fail to bring the person into a relationship with the Savior. It is encouraging, therefore, to remember that the Holy Spirit "convinces the world of sin."

Repentance as Sorrow for Sin

In genuine repentance there also is a *godly sorrow* for the fact of one's sin. Some people recognize what they have done and even accept responsibility for their actions, but have a "So what?" attitude. They feel no regret or sorrow over what they have done.

The word "repent," however, means that there is genuine regret, pain, and sorrow for sin. In Psalm 51, this emotional element is inescapable. It permeates every sentence. David frequently requests the restoration of joy (vv. 8, 12), and he commends a broken and contrite heart and spirit as acceptable to the Lord (v. 17).

If sorrow is to be effective, it must be more than mere remorse. It must be the right kind of remorse, regret for the right reason. We can be sorry for our sins because of the unfortunate consequences. This, however, is not real repentance. The wrong kind of repentance is regret, not for what we have done, but that we were *caught*. Real repentance means knowing that what I have done is really wrong and an offense against God. It is wrong because it grieves the Lord. Something is right or wrong, not because of our feelings, but because of a relationship to the will of the Lord. This is an important distinction. For years we have heard that "crime does not pay" and that consequently we should be law-abiding. But some people have found that crime does pay—and quite handsomely at that. The motivation for living by the law should not be that crime leads to unpleasant consequences. The motivation should be that crime is wrong.

This is the difference between genuine repentance and an apparent repentance that we might call mere penitence. In true repentance a real sense of regret is present, a contrition, or godly sorrow over sin. A child may be told by his mother that he is not to take cookies from the cookie jar while she is gone. His appetite wins and he eats two or three cookies. When his mother discovers what he has done, she spanks the boy. As he considers the aching part of his anatomy he is sorry for what he has done. But he is not sorry for doing wrong but for being punished. If he could do it again and somehow be assured that he would not be caught and punished, he would eat the cookies. The test of our repentance is whether or not we have a genuine godly sorrow for our sin.

David felt this godly sorrow. Note what he said of his sin: "Against Thee, Thee only, I have sinned, and done what is evil in Thy sight" (Ps. 51:4). When Nathan identified his sin for him, David repented (2 Sam. 12:13)—after the pronouncement of the curse, but before it was carried out. His repentance appears to have been genuine, rather than a mere reaction because of the pain he had brought upon himself.

Repentance as Resolve to Change

Genuine repentance produces a resolve to change. This is part of the difference between the two words for repentance in each of the Testaments. One conveys the idea of merely feeling deeply and being concerned about what one has done. This, however, may or may not lead to a change of conduct. Real repentance produces an alteration in our ways. The word that conveys this idea means literally "to think differently, to be of a different mind."

This sharp distinction between the two Greek words for repentance is seen clearly in Paul's statement in 2 Corinthians 7:8–10:

> For though I caused you sorrow by my letter, I do not regret it; though I did regret it,—for I see that that letter caused you sorrow, though only for a while—I now rejoice, not that you were made sorrowful, but that you were made sorrowful to the point of repentance; for you were made sorrowful according to the will of God, in order that you might not suffer loss in anything through us. For the sorrow that is according to the will of God produces a repentance without regret, leading to salvation; but the sorrow of the world produces death.

This contrast in concepts is also found in two other New Testament passages. Some have wondered why Judas repented but was never restored. Was his sin so hideous that God would not forgive him? Was what he did really so much worse, after all, than what Peter did in denying his Lord? Certainly Peter received forgiveness; why, then, should not Judas? In particular, we may contrast Acts 2:37–41, where thousands repented and were baptized, with Matthew 27:3–5, where Judas repented and hanged himself. In each case, the reaction seems to be treated as the appropriate response.

The key lies in the two different words in the passages. The Matthew text says that Judas felt sorrow or remorse for his actions, but nothing more. The word Peter used in his sermon at Pentecost shows the need for a complete, radical change of thinking. The new believers reversed their thinking and resolved to demonstrate their sincerity by their outward actions. Thus real repentance includes all three factors: recognizing the nature of the sin and accepting responsibility for it (the intellectual element); feeling godly sorrow for having wronged God (the emotional element); and determining to change one's action (the volitional element).

True repentance will not allow us to be continually morbid, moping over our past sins. Resolve puts that away. Real repentance, including a genuine turning from sin, brings forgiveness and consequent peace.

An early Christian tradition says that on one occasion after Pentecost, Peter heard a rooster crow during his sermon. According to the story, Peter remembered how he had earlier denied the Lord and those memories so overwhelmed him that he was unable to continue preaching.

Another tradition also describes Peter hearing a cock crow during his sermon. He remembered how he had denied the Lord before, and determined that he would not repeat that failure. He preached as he had never preached before. That tradition has no stronger historical support than the first, but I can at least consider the second story as possible. It fits in with what I know of Peter and his overall experience. Real repentance, because it is a break with the past sin, also puts an end to any continuing remorse for sin.

The Importance of the Repentance Message

We can catch the importance of repentance in the frequency and emphasis of references to it in the New Testament. As we observed earlier, the opening note of John the Baptist's preparatory message emphasized this theme: "Repent, for the kingdom of heaven is at hand" (Matt. 3:2). Judgment was coming. In light of this, John called for radical transformation. His hearers were to bring forth fruit worthy of repentance (Luke 3:8).

When asked what to do, John specified actions appropriate to each of the subgroups of his hearers. He told them to abandon their old ways and to sincerely believe. To the multitudes he said, "Let the man who has two tunics share with him who has none; and let him who has food do likewise" (Luke 3:11). The tax collectors who came for baptism were told, "Collect no more than what you have been ordered to" (v. 13). Soldiers were told, "Do not take money from anyone by force, or accuse anyone falsely, and be content with your wages" (v. 14).

Jesus proclaimed this same theme: "Repent, for the kingdom of heaven is at hand" (Matt. 4:17). Not only was this concept prominent in Jesus' own teaching, but it was the focus of the disciples' message as well. "And they went out and preached that men should repent" (Mark 6:12). Similarly the seventy called upon their hearers to repent. The one ground of condemnation of Chorazin, Bethsaida, and Capernaum was that they did not repent. Had the mighty works done in them been done in Tyre and Sidon, these two towns would long before have repented in sackcloth and ashes (Luke 10:13–15). The men of Nineveh would arise at the judgment of this generation and condemn it, for they repented at the preaching of Jonah, but this evil generation had evidently not repented, even though One greater than Jonah was there (Luke 11:29–31).

From the incident in Nineveh, we see the necessary connection between repentance and certain actions that demonstrate the reality of that repentance. The king of Nineveh wore sackcloth and sat in ashes. He commanded his subjects to do so, and told them to cry mightily to God, and to turn from their evil ways and violence (Jonah 3). Thus, repentance was demonstrated by a change of mind and action.

Repentance was also emphasized in the apostolic preaching. Peter preached repentance on every important occasion: on Pentecost (Acts 2:38), to the crowd in Solomon's porch (Acts 3:19), before the Sanhedrin (Acts 5:31), and to Simon Magus (Acts 8:22). The Apostle's message also included a call to demonstrate the sincerity of repentance by the outward act of baptism (Acts 2:38; cf. Acts 10:47–48). Paul, in his first preaching, linked his message with John's preaching of repentance (Acts 13:24), and told the group at Mars Hill: "Therefore having overlooked the times of ignorance, God is now declaring to men that all everywhere should repent" (Acts 17:30).

Because of the emphasis on repentance in the preaching of the gospel, it cannot be neglected in our understanding of salvation. This is particularly important in our day. The strong emphasis being placed on *positive thinking* can easily lead us to avoid such "negative" ideas as sin, conviction, and repentance. We have also heard about the dangers of preoccupation with irrational and inappropriate feelings of guilt. Yet, if we are really guilty, it is essential that we recognize it and repent of our sin.

This recognition makes a big difference in the depth and reality of Christian experience at later stages of the salvation process. The Pharisee Simon was critical of Jesus for letting a sinful woman touch him in the process of washing, wiping, kissing, and anointing his feet (Luke 7:36–50). Jesus said to him: "He who is forgiven little, loves little" (v. 47). Repentance leads to an awareness that we have been forgiven. It produces a deep love for the Lord, following repentance. If we want wholehearted and intensive Christian discipleship, then we must have the proper biblical emphasis on repentance.

Study Guide

Key Questions

1. How are repentance and faith mutually interdependent?
2. Repentance means turning away from one's sins. What would this definition indicate for people who contend that "once saved, always saved; therefore, I can continue to live as I please"?
3. We often rationalize to try to explain or cover up our sin. Who were the characters the author used as examples? Can you think of other characters from the Bible who also rationalized their sin?
4. Why is it important to realize that the Holy Spirit is the one who convicts the world of sin (John 16:8)?
5. What are three characteristics of real repentance?

Bible Investigation

1. Matthew 3:1–2 speaks of John the Baptist's message of repentance. How did both repentance and

faith become part of John's message? (See Matt. 3:11–12; Mark 1:7–8; Luke 3:15–18; John 1:6–35; 3:27–30; 5:33–36).

2. Sorrow for wrongdoing is true repentance, not sorrow because of being caught. Psalm 51:4, 17 suggests that sin is committed mainly against God, even though others are also hurt. What do you think David meant by these words, spoken in contrition over his sin against Bathsheba and Uriah?

Personal Application

1. One of the Hebrew words for repentance is an onomatopoeic word, which means its sound suggests its meaning. Its literal meaning is to sigh, pant, or groan. What does this suggest to us about our personal emotions as related to our own sin? Can you think of some personal sin over which you sighed or groaned?

2. Perhaps you know Christians who live in the "I'm a sinner" mode. Is this the way Christians should be, or is there more to consider than self-effacement? What is the correct self-image for a Christian?

For Further Thought

1. The line "Love means never having to say you're sorry" from the movie *Love Story*, has become famous. Is there any biblical precept to support such an idea? What might Christians say that love means (using love as the agape form)?

2. The power of positive thinking sometimes gets mixed up in the gospel message. Does it have anything to do with the repentance/faith requisites for salvation? Where, if anywhere, does it fit into the Christian's life?

4

Believing Is Seeing

"Faith is believing what you know ain't so," Mark Twain once said. "Seeing is believing," says the world. But for the Christian "believing is seeing" is a more accurate understanding of faith. John put it this way: "But as many as received Him, to them He gave the right to become children of God, even to those who believe in His name" (John 1:12). Faith is the means by which the believer experiences the ultimate reality. For the Christian, believing is seeing.

"For by grace are you saved through faith," wrote Paul to the Ephesians (2:8, KJV). Faith is one of the two basic elements in conversion, the other being repentance.

The Relation of Faith and Repentance

Faith and repentance are not the same thing, but two parts of the same process or two perspectives on the same event. Repentance is turning away from one's sins, repudiating them, abandoning them. Faith, on the other hand, is turning to Christ, accepting him, committing oneself to him. If conversion is turning from sin to Christ, the movement away from sin is repentance, while the movement toward Christ is faith.

Faith and repentance stimulate one another to a spontaneous reaction. One repents of sin not primarily because of a distaste for sin, but because of what one believes about God and Christ. One consequently sees the wrong in this sin, in relationship to God's perfection and requirements. In the same way, faith is motivated by one's recognition of one's own sinfulness and inability to break the pattern of evil. It is necessary to place one's trust in Christ for transformation. We cannot think of either faith or repentance as logically prior to the other, but we should conceive of them as interrelated.

Faith basically is wholehearted trust in Christ for forgiveness and salvation. The Greek word commonly used for faith comes from a verb meaning "to persuade." Thus, faith refers to a state of persuasion or conviction, a settled condition of soul. There are several elements involved in faith.

Faith as Belief

The first factor is believing something to be true, or "believing that." This is the general sense of faith, a dimension that saving faith shares with other kinds of faith, both religious and secular. The Bible makes clear that believing in certain truths is necessary for salvation. The writer of Hebrews asserted: "And without faith it is impossible to please Him, for he who comes to God must believe that He is, and that He is a rewarder of those who seek Him" (11:6). Belief in God's existence and at least this one attribute of his character needs to be present, or we would not even approach him.

Jesus also was concerned about what humans thought of him. Warmth of feeling and depth of commitment to him were insufficient in themselves. The concept persons held regarding him was the deciding factor. Thus he asked his disciples, "Who do people say that the Son of Man is?" They told him that many opinions were held. This did not end Jesus' inquiry. He pressed them for a declaration of their own convictions. When Peter answered, "Thou art the Christ, the Son of the living God," Jesus responded, "Blessed are you, Simon Barjona, because flesh and blood did not reveal this to you, but My Father who is in heaven!" Only then did he indicate that he would build his church upon this rock, and that he would give the keys of the kingdom of heaven and the authority of binding and loosing (Matt. 16:13–20). Belief in the deity and saving work of Jesus is apparently essential for a proper relationship with him.

The second ingredient in saving faith is the belief that Jesus is the unique God-man. He is not some weak-willed human suffering from delusions of grandeur—but *the* God-man. If we do not accept the complete humanity of Jesus along with his deity, conversion is worthless. Only a perfect man could pay for the sins of the human race. Jesus Christ is the perfect One, the God-man.

Accepting Jesus' humanity was a problem for the recipients of John's first letter. False teachers claimed to present a higher knowledge of spiritual truth than that accepted by the average Christian. In particular, they denied the genuine humanity of Jesus Christ. They held that the material or physical realm is not only less real than the intellectual or spiritual realm, but morally inferior as well. Thus all that is physical, including our bodies, is evil. This means Jesus could not really have taken a physical body. His apparent humanity was only that: apparent. His body was only an illusion. His physical nature was something like a projected three-dimensional picture. He was more like a ghost than a human.

The *virgin* birth was no problem, but the virgin *birth* was a real obstacle. Mary contributed nothing to Jesus. He passed through her like water through a tube.

John confidently affirmed Jesus' full humanity. Urging his hearers to "test the spirits" because many false prophets have gone out into the world, he wrote: "By this you know the Spirit of God: every spirit that confesses that Jesus Christ has come in the flesh is from God; and every spirit that does not confess Jesus is not from God" (1 John 4:2–3). He also added, "Whoever believes that Jesus is the Christ is born of God; and whoever loves the Father loves the child born of Him" (5:1). Belief in the full humanity, John argues, is essential for a proper relationship to Christ and to God.

The Apostles also included belief in the resurrection as part of the intellectual dimension of the Christian faith. Paul wrote, "If you confess with your mouth Jesus as Lord, and believe in your heart that God raised Him from the dead, you shall be saved; for with the heart man believes, resulting in righteousness, and with the mouth he confesses, resulting in salvation" (Rom. 10:9–10).

While intellectual assent is not in itself sufficient for salvation, it is nonetheless necessary. This emphasis is needed in an age that stresses feelings and tends to downplay intellectual belief. Sometimes we hear expressions of faith such as "Jesus is the greatest." Jesus certainly is "the greatest," but our Lord required more specific belief about his own person and work. Intellectual assent is an indispensable part of faith because, as important as trusting a person is, it is more important that the right person be trusted.

There are many competitors for the religious allegiance of would-be believers today. Each has its own object of faith, its own prophet or teacher. In light of this, we must remember that in the Bible faith is not a blind commitment to someone or something, nor can it be today.

In normal human experience, we do not separate trust in a person from some elementary beliefs about that person. Commitment to a husband or wife is not primarily intellectual belief, but there is at least an implicit belief about the person. Before a man embraces his wife, he doesn't run down an elaborate checklist to identify the right woman: "Let's see—five feet four, 120 pounds, blond hair, blue eyes, small scar on left cheek—that's my wife, all right." He knows however, by at least a glance that this is indeed his wife. He doesn't embrace just any woman he meets. His identification of his wife rests on basic facts about who this person is.

Similarly, we don't approach a stranger, give him $200 cash, and ask him to deposit it in the bank for us. We would choose a friend, determine that this individual is indeed that friend, and that she can be trusted. If we were in a desperate situation and had to call on a stranger for such a service, we would surely attempt some hasty assessment of his or her trustworthiness.

My point is this: It isn't faith itself that saves us. Faith is merely the means or the instrument by which we receive salvation. It is Christ who saves us, and our faith must be in him. In our day we hear such varied declarations about belief that we might get the impression that faith itself accomplishes something. We must have, it seems, "faith in faith." But this is not the biblical idea. In Scripture faith is the instrument for laying hold of God's working; it is God himself and God alone who produces the results.

Faith as Trust

As important as faith is, believing the wrong thing is disastrous. Mere creedal belief is ineffectual. Perhaps the most pointed biblical statement of this truth is in James 2:19: "You believe that God is one. You do well; the demons also believe, and shudder." Mere intellectual assent alone fails to lead to saving faith. Demons are not saved! Someone could argue that the problem for demons is not the improper kind of faith, but an inadequate form of that faith. Bare monotheism is not enough. The context of James 2:19 indicates, however, that it is not the content of the creed but the type of faith that makes it unacceptable.

Saving faith, in the biblical sense, is not simply *believing that* or intellectual assent. It is *belief in*—trust and commitment to a person. In many biblical texts the word *trust* is virtually interchangeable with *faith.* One of these is Hebrews 6:18–20: "In order that by two unchangeable things, in which it is impossible for God to lie, we may have strong encouragement, we who have fled for refuge in laying hold of the hope set before us. This hope we have as an anchor of the soul, a hope both sure and steadfast and one which enters within the veil, where Jesus has entered as a forerunner for us, having become a high priest forever according to the order of Melchizedek."

This personal dimension of faith is clearly revealed in the use of *believe,* together with a preposition such as *in* or *upon.* We find numerous examples of this in the New Testament. Jesus said, "Let not your heart be troubled; believe in God [or, you believe in God], believe also in Me" (John 14:1). Paul said, "But for our sake also, to whom it will be reckoned, as those who believe in Him who raised Jesus our Lord from the dead" (Rom. 4:24). John wrote of those who receive him (John 1:12) and assured his readers that eternal life is given to those who "believe in him" (John 3:15–16, 18). Paul answered the Philippian jailor's question, "What must I do to be saved?" with "Believe in the Lord Jesus, and you shall be saved" (Acts 16:31).

We can find many illustrations of this idea of trust. To me, marriage is perhaps the most complete and accurate picture of trust. We can believe a great deal about another person. We can accept the fact that he or she is a fine man or woman, and would make an excellent spouse. We can even declare this verbally. Real faith in the other person, however, will only be fully demonstrated as we take that step of commitment, by accepting that person as our husband or wife.

Faith and Understanding

Faith does not have to be complete or perfect for God to act. An instructive example of this is found in Matthew 9:20–22, in the story about the woman who touched the fringe of Jesus' garment. Her understanding was far from complete. She probably knew little of what we would call the doctrine of the person of Christ. Certainly her understanding was less than that of the disciples. She simply believed that Jesus had the ability to heal her of the hemorrhage that had afflicted her for so many years. Her *faith* bordered on superstition: "If I just touch His garments, I shall get well" (Mark 5:28). Yet, faulty though her belief was, she was healed. She acted on what she knew about Jesus. This is an encouragement to us. A perfectly developed theology is not essential for salvation.

It is doubtful that at the time of their salvation the disciples had a doctrine of Jesus' person and work close to our own. We know that Old Testament believers had only a dim vision of the Messiah. They certainly believed that God was holy and righteous, that they were sinners incapable of fulfilling the requirements of God revealed in the Law, and thus of pleasing him or attaining his favor by their own efforts. They also believed in God's graciousness: that he would provide for their salvation if they simply abandoned themselves to his mercy. But they did not know the details of Jesus' life, or even his name. It isn't clear that they understood that God's provision of salvation would take place through an individual. Nonetheless, they had the basic contour of faith and so were saved, though lacking some of the details of its content.

All of this means that saving faith is a genuine possibility even for a child who may have a rather limited understanding of the plan of salvation. Faith is wholehearted response to God based on the knowledge we have. There is a vast difference, however, between limited understanding of revealed truth and the denial or rejection of truths once learned.

Faith and Doubt

There also is room for incomplete certainty in faith. Some of us occasionally find that an element of doubt intrudes into our faith. A man came to Jesus asking him to heal his demon-possessed son (Mark 9:14–29). Jesus said to him, "All things are possible to him who believes" (v. 23). The response of this man expressed the struggle in his soul: "I do believe; help me in my unbelief" (v. 24). He recognized that he believed, but not perfectly and single-mindedly, and he wanted his belief made perfect. Jesus honored that strong element of faith by healing the son. We may also find ourselves in this man's situation. While confessing our faith, we may find it necessary to pray for an increase of that faith. This is an honorable request, and one that the Lord will grant.

We should note the nature of doubt and its relationship to faith, as well as the way Jesus dealt with doubters. In Luke 7:18–23 we find an account from the life of John the Baptist. Imprisoned, John began to wonder if Jesus was really the one he should believe in. He sent his disciples to Jesus to ask him about this. John's action reveals his doubt, not his unbelief. His problem was uncertainty, rather than rejection of Jesus' claims.

Doubt bears the same relationship to unbelief as temptation does to sin. Doubt is not itself unbelief; it is simply the occasion that may lead to unbelief. On the other hand, it may also lead to a stronger faith. John's doubt shouldn't surprise us. He sensed that he was about to forfeit his life for his commitment. In view of the high stakes involved, the Baptizer needed greater assurance for his faith than would normally be the case.

The way Jesus dealt with John is noteworthy. He didn't rebuke him for his lack of faith, or manipulate him with threats and coaxings, or deliver a dogmatic authoritarian statement, "I am the One! You must believe me!" Jesus responded by pointing out to John's disciples what he was doing, and sending them back to John to report these evidences. He let John decide for himself, but gave him adequate evidence for belief. His words of commendation (Luke 7:28) suggest that John's response was positive.

Jesus handled Thomas's skepticism in much the same way. Thomas doubted the first reports of Jesus' resurrection. Before he would believe, he said, he must see and even feel the nail prints in Jesus' hands and the sword wound in his side. Jesus rebuked his unwillingness to believe without seeing. This was no commendation of blind faith, for Thomas had other grounds for faith: his past experience with the Lord, including knowledge of his words and deeds, and the testimony of the disciples, who were trustworthy men. Nevertheless, Jesus condescended to provide Thomas with additional evidence. He showed him his pierced hands and side (John 20:24–29).

These examples challenge some of the misconceptions surrounding the intellectual status of Christianity. One idea claims that faith is little more than superstition. Faith, however, is not belief in the absurd. While faith cannot offer proof beyond all doubt, it does provide evidence to support its claims. To a view that limits *proof* to evidence demonstrated by sense perception, Christianity seems irrational. Such a position, however, is itself a faith statement, and all of us have areas of our lives that are not restricted to sense experiences.

Sometimes faith is contrasted with knowledge, as if faith were the opposite of knowledge, or at best something less than knowledge. Such a view means the scientist has knowledge; the Christian believer has only faith.

Two observations are important here. First, all knowledge includes an element of faith—if by *faith* we mean a belief for which there is no absolute advance proof. Every reasoning process involves some assumptions. Once we make these we can reason from the starting point and then see the sensibility of the position. As Anselm, the medieval scholar, put it in his approach to the Christian faith, it is a matter of "faith seeking understanding." This is true not only of belief in the Christian gospel, but of other views of life as well. It is not faith versus reason, but one faith versus another.

Second, faith is not necessarily less than knowledge. It is possible to believe with such certainty that the belief could be classified as knowledge, without that belief reaching the point of trust. Faith is not inferior to uncommitted knowledge; it is superior to it.

Faith and Works

Finally, we need to see the relationship of faith to works. As we will note numerous times in this book, faith rather than works is the basis of salvation. Sometimes, however, faith is construed as if it were the one good work a person does. This is not the picture given by Scripture. It appears that faith, our response to God's action, is itself a gift of God. In Ephesians 2:9, "that" which is spoken of as the gift of God, not of works, is evidently the whole process, faith as well as grace.

Genuine faith distinguishes itself from false faith by commitment. True faith leads to obedience. It will not remain inactive. As James wrote, while faith without works is dead, real faith proves it is alive by producing works (James 2:17–18). Works are the smoke that proves that the fire of faith is present. Just as no amount of smoke will produce fire, so no amount of works will make faith. But where faith is present, works will appear as well.

Study Guide

Key Questions

1. Peter's profession that Jesus was the Christ, the Son of the living God, evoked a response from Jesus. What was it, and how significant was it?
2. Why is it imperative that we believe in the God-man, Jesus? Note John's words in 1 John 3:23; 5:1.
3. Why is "Just have faith" an incomplete answer for the way of salvation?
4. How does the author say marriage illustrates trust for us as it relates to our trust in Jesus?
5. What is the mark of genuine faith according to the author? How does James confirm this (James 2:14–26)?

Bible Investigation

1. Do Ephesians 2:8–9 and James 2:17–18 need reconciling or blending for us to understand the true pic-

ture of faith? Read Ephesians 2:10 and James 2:14–26 for a sound understanding of faith and works.

2. The author discusses Jesus' relationship with doubting Thomas and the imprisoned John the Baptist. Are there Old Testament characters who also had distrust or doubting problems? Read Jonah and Matthew 26.

3. In Ephesians 4:11–16, Paul talks about the church as a body and its members' various gifts. The goal for believers is works of service that lead to unity and maturity in the faith. What do you think these works might be and how do they bring about unity and maturity?

Personal Application

1. If we should doubt our faith, what would be some good Bible passages to read?

2. Do doubts sometimes arise because our emotions are not consistent with what we think Christians ought to feel? How can we help ourselves or others work through this problem?

For Further Thought

1. How widespread do you think doubting is among Christians? If a person has intellectual doubts, how would you respond? What kinds of doubts do you think might be common?

2. Matthew 26:59–60 says the members of the Sanhedrin were looking for false evidence against Jesus but did not find any, though there were many false witnesses. Do you think sometimes we could really be looking for excuses to doubt? If so, we need to find the reasons why we want to doubt. What might they be?

5

Out of Debt

The young clergyman suffered from severe guilt. More than anything else he wanted to be right with God and at peace with him. But that peace consistently eluded him. He believed if he could do enough good works, it would balance his account with God by cancelling each sin with a corresponding good deed.

He used every available means to this end. To the standard routine of praying seven times daily, he added his own rigors and vigils. He fasted, sometimes for three days at a time, totally without food. He deprived himself of the warmth of blankets. He searched his memory for every unconfessed sin, and disclosed these in the confessional, sometimes for up to six hours. He traveled to Rome, visiting the religious shrines and relics there, hoping to gain merit with God. But peace eluded him. How could anyone ever accumulate enough goodness to nullify his or her sin? It seemed as if God only disapproved and condemned him. God was just. That meant that he could not overlook any wrong done by man, no matter how trivial.

This man's problem disturbed his religious community. His excessive introspection and morbidity made other members uneasy. Confessors grew impatient hearing about his countless insignificant acts. Finally, his superior found a solution. He would work the young man so hard that he had no time for self-examination. He would study for a doctor's degree. He would preach regularly. And he would become a professor of Bible in the university.

The solution proved effective, but not in the way the superior intended. As the young man immersed himself in studies, he made some amazing discoveries. He found, from Psalm 22, that Jesus also experienced the sense of despair and rejection by God that he was undergoing. And he learned from Paul's writings that justice can have two meanings: either strict enforcement of the Law and its demands, or *justification*, the process of forgiving, suspending sentence, and pronouncing the person righteous. Joy leaped in his heart as he realized that justification is not something a human being achieves. Rather, it is God's gift, and the human simply accepts it by faith.

That man was Martin Luther, and his rediscovery of the biblical doctrine of justification by grace became the basis of the Protestant Reformation and evangelical faith ever since. It is the answer to the question, "How can a perfectly holy God accept a sinful human?"

Justification as Righteous Status before God

Justification involves a basic change in the status of one's relationship with God. It is God's act whereby he takes a sinful, guilty, and condemned human, and regards him or her as no longer guilty. It is a declarative act, involving a change of status, not of condition. It does not necessarily make a person good. The change is in the way God regards the sinner.

Two meanings of the word *righteous* need to be distinguished here. One refers to the state of goodness or rightness. If I have perfectly fulfilled a particular law, or at least have not violated it, I am righteous. Nothing more can be demanded of me. I have measured up to the requirements.

The second meaning of *righteous* involves some deviation from the standards, resulting in guilt. This guilt requires punishment. Such guilt, however, can be removed, either by payment of the penalty or by cancellation of the debt. When this is done the transgressor is righteous. Both persons—the one who has done no wrong and the one who has done wrong and now "paid his debt"—are equally righteous. Nothing further can be required of either.

It is this second sense of the word *righteous* that is involved in justification. No one is righteous in the first sense. No one is innocent before God. The Bible makes clear in numerous passages, such as Romans 3:23, that all have sinned and are therefore guilty. When God declares a person just or righteous, it is not because the penalty has been abolished. Rather, it is because the sentence has been fulfilled, and the believer stands righteous before the Law.

No one is justified by fulfilling the Law. One popular theory claims that although no one is innocent, we can be justified by our actions. Therefore, if we do enough good deeds, they will cancel our sins. But we were required to do those good deeds anyway, so we cannot apply the extra value to our failures.

Suppose you are driving your car and your mind is wandering. As a result, you inadvertently fail to stop at a stop sign. Soon a police car with a flashing light appears. The officer motions you to pull over and informs you of your offense. What would your reply be?

You might justify yourself by explaining that you always stop for stop signs. You have obeyed the law in many similar situations. Doesn't that count for something?

"No," the officer would reply. "You were only doing what you were supposed to do in those instances. In this case, you failed to do that."

But you object, "I sometimes stop even where there is no stop sign. Doesn't that make a difference?"

The officer replies, "All of that is very commendable. But we're not concerned with those cases. It's *this* stop sign that's the problem. And nothing can change the fact that you failed to stop this time."

So it is with our relationship to God. We cannot do more than fulfill what is required of us in any matter, and there are always other matters we fail to fulfill.

Paul put it quite directly: "A man is not justified by the works of the Law but through faith in Christ Jesus, even we have believed in Christ Jesus, that we may be justified by faith in Christ, and not by works of the Law, since by the works of the Law shall no flesh be justified" (Gal. 2:16).

Jesus made the point somewhat differently. Some people thought that they only had to fulfill the Law and they would be righteous. One of these was the rich young man who came to Jesus (Mark 10:17–22). He wanted to know how to inherit eternal life. All his life he had kept the commandments. But he lacked one thing. Jesus told him to sell his possessions and give them to the poor. This he was unwilling to do. He was too attached to his wealth to give it up. In the same way, no one is capable of reaching God's standard on his or her own because God demands perfection.

Justification as Reception of Christ's Righteousness

The act of God is one of *declaring* a person righteous, rather than *making* him or her good or holy. Justification does not transfer goodness into a person. It is a declarative act or, as it is sometimes termed, a forensic act. It is a pronouncement of the status of a person.

Numerous biblical passages teach this truth. A prominent one is Romans 8:33–34. Here the idea of God justifying is contrasted with condemning or accusing. To condemn doesn't mean making a person wicked, sinful, or evil. It is a declaration that the person is already in this condition. Similarly, justification is not a matter of making the person good. It is a declaration that he or she is acquitted. It is God's response to the charge of unrighteousness brought against the individual. God both condemns the unjust and justifies the righteous. In each case, it is an act of pronouncement, not of transformation. There is an alteration in the person, but it is called regeneration, not justification.

Here we find a puzzle. If justification is God's declaration of our human status, and if no one is as perfect as God requires, how can God say, "Good enough!"? Either he must be mistaken in his appraisal or dishonest in his judgment.

The solution to this puzzle is that justification is more than a two-party relationship. If it were just God and I, then I would fail to meet with God's approval. Justification, however, is a three-party transaction, involving God, Jesus, and me. God sees me, but not with my righteousness alone. He sees me with Christ's. Jesus' death is so highly valued because it was voluntary. He gave up his life freely. Consequently, part of his righteousness can be credited to me. It is as if I owe a debt that I am unable to pay. All my efforts to hide my indebtedness are useless. But then a concerned third party with abundant assets offers to pay the debt for me. Now I am "paid up" with my creditor. Thus God's declaration of my righteousness is based on my actual standing, the righteousness that I genuinely possess, even though it is not my own accomplishment.

Some people may feel that there is something wrong with this process because someone else supplies something I need. Note, however, that this would only be wrong if it were not agreed on by all parties involved. I do not take from Christ something that he does not give. Nor does God extract some act of obedience from his reluctant Son. All parties have consented to the agreement.

This means that the recipient must also consent. The crediting of Christ's righteousness to the sinner is not automatic. Unless each person accepts it, the righteousness of Christ means nothing to that individual. Several years ago, a convicted criminal had served part of his sentence when the state governor offered him a pardon. The man refused! State law officials were confused about what they should do. The matter was settled in court, and the court ruled that a convicted criminal cannot be pardoned against his will. So the man served his sentence. Despite the will of God to pardon or justify all human beings (2 Peter 3:9), many persons are condemned (Rom. 6:23)—simply because they will not accept Christ's pardon.

God makes sinners righteous. He doesn't merely announce our righteous status. He actually gives us righteousness—not by filling us with so much goodness that we fulfill the Law, but by giving us the gift of righteousness accomplished by Jesus Christ. We see this in Paul's statement: "For as through one man's disobedience the many were made sinners, even so through the obedience of the One the many will be made righteous" (Rom. 5:19).

Justification as God's Gift

Salvation is by grace and is a free gift. We don't earn it or qualify for it. It must be given by God. He offers it freely because he loves us and is generous. "For by grace you have been saved through faith; and that not of yourselves, it is the gift of God; not as a result of works, that no one should boast" (Eph. 2:8–9).

These verses also indicate the way salvation is energized by faith. It is not by works, or faith plus works. It is faith, period. As we noted elsewhere in this volume, faith means believing that God has prepared this salvation on our behalf, and then accepting his offer. Salvation, then, is not "on account of" faith. It is literally "out of" faith. Faith is not a good work. It is a gift of God.

This has always been God's way of justifying persons, at all times and in all places. Some Christians have argued that in the era before Christ, people were justified by actually *being just:* by perfectly fulfilling the demands of the Law. Two considerations, however, one negative and one positive, rule that out.

The negative argument is the biblical statement that no one is saved by works of the Law. This statement has neither temporal nor geographical restrictions. If it is impossible now to be justified by fulfilling the Law, and it could not be done in New Testament times, then it was not a possibility in the Old Testament period either.

The positive argument is the evidence from Scripture of people who were justified on the basis of faith. Abraham is often pictured as the paragon of Old Testament godliness. Yet the Bible makes it clear that Abraham's righteousness before God was because of his faith. In Galatians 3:5–6 Paul linked Abraham with his own readers; "Does He then who provides you with the Spirit and works miracles among you, do it by the works of the Law, or by hearing with faith? Even so Abraham 'believed God and it was reckoned to him as righteousness.'" Even Abel is identified this way: "By faith Abel offered to God a better sacrifice than Cain, through which he obtained the testimony that he was righteous, God testifying about his gifts" (Heb. 11:4). The writer did not say that because Abel had faith, he was capable of good works and his works made him righteous. Rather, because Abel had faith, he was considered righteous, and as a believer he offered his sacrifice. God's acceptance of the sacrifice was evidence of Abel's justification in God's sight, but the sacrifice had no inherent value.

This idea of justification purely by grace is difficult to accept, or even to comprehend. Somehow the idea that God should accept me and forgive me, without my doing something in return or suffering at least a bit, does not seem right. This is because one of the most fundamental elements in sinful human nature is independence. We want to say we have achieved what is ours, at least in part. Another factor is a mistaken sense of justice. It is fine for God to freely forgive *me.* But that this other person, who has lived a life of sin for years and perhaps has wronged me—that she should not be punished hardly seems right. Ultimately, however, it is God who is the controller of justice, and it is he alone against whom we sin (Ps. 51:4). If he says, "Forgiven!" then I am not in a position to insist that there be retribution.

Our willingness to accept God's gift of grace is an error, but there is also another danger we face. It is presuming upon grace. I may say, "Since God justifies me by his grace it doesn't matter how I live. I shouldn't try to be good enough to please him. I can simply come to him claiming his justification and forgiveness." Paul knew some who said, "Let us continue in sin that grace may abound" (Rom. 6:1). Would it not be more to God's glory if he had even more opportunity to forgive? Paul sternly rejected this idea: "May it never be! How shall we who died to sin still live in it? . . . What then? Shall we sin because we are not under law but under grace? May it never be!" (vv. 2, 15).

Justification comes only to those who have been truly converted. A genuine turning from sin precludes continuing in it. Similarly, all who have really experienced divine grace will respond to God's commands. The Christian does not receive "cheap grace." While justification by grace is free, it is not cheap. It is extremely costly, in terms of what God gave.

Justification and Sin's Temporal Consequences

Sometimes we hear justification defined as "just as if I had never sinned." There is an element of truth in this definition, but it can also be misleading. It's true that the status of justified sinners is the same as if they had never sinned. They have no guilt, no penalty, no liability to punishment, any more than if they had never committed a sin. No condemnation remains.

In another sense, however, this isn't so. The eternal and spiritual effects of sin are totally cancelled, but certain temporal and natural effects linger. Even God does not erase the effects of the past. Life will never be as though the sin had never happened. Sin sets in motion certain "natural" causes. Ordinarily God does not introduce a miracle to nullify this course of events.

An example of this is found in certain tragic aspects of David's sin. When David saw and desired Bathsheba, he took her and committed adultery. Then in order to cover that sin, he committed another sin, murder. When Nathan the prophet came and revealed David's sin to him, he repented (2 Sam. 12:13). He was assured that God forgave him: "The LORD also has taken away your sin; you shall not die" (v. 13). Despite this, however, certain results persisted. Nathan informed David of one of these: "However, because by this deed you have given occasion to the enemies of the LORD to blaspheme, the child also that is born to you shall surely die" (v. 14). And so it was. The sin no longer condemned David, but there were unfortunate temporal results.

Certain other dire prophecies were also pronounced by God: David's house would experience violence and killing. His wives would be taken by another man, just as he had taken Uriah's wife (2 Sam. 12:10–11). All of this came to pass. David's son Amnon raped his half sister, Tamar (2 Sam. 13:1–19). Her brother Absalom retaliated by killing Amnon (2 Sam. 13:20–29). Then Absalom raised a conspiracy of rebellion against David (2 Sam. 15) and slept with David's concubines (2 Sam. 16:20–23). Finally Absalom was killed. The temporal consequences of sin ran throughout the course of David's life.

So it is with sin today. We may have complete forgiveness and remission of the eternal consequences of sin, yet the temporal results linger. We should not think of this as incomplete justification. Rather, it is a sobering reminder of the seriousness of sin. Sin is not something we can trifle with. I am judicially forgiven, but I cannot remove myself from sin's temporal consequences.

Imagine a thief who is apprehended in the midst of committing a crime. He is seriously injured by a gunshot wound that requires the amputation of his arm. While serving his sentence in prison he becomes a Christian. His sin is forgiven and the condemnation removed. God, however, does not promise to restore the arm. The man goes through life suffering the affliction caused by his sin. Thousands of people whose sin has been forgiven and remitted must still live with the fact that their families have been virtually destroyed by sin. Sin is a serious matter indeed.

Yet what a glorious truth: We, unrighteous, wicked people that we are, can stand before God, fully accepted as righteous with him. That is an amazing, breathtaking truth. Small wonder that the song writer penned:

> Now my heart condemns me not,
> pure before the law I stand;
> He who cleansed me from all spot,
> satisfied its last demand.

Study Guide

Key Questions

1. What was it that bothered young Martin Luther so much? How did his biblical studies eventually lead to the Reformation? Why is this significant for us today?
2. If no one is righteous (Rom. 3:10), how do we become righteous in God's eyes?
3. Sometimes after a sinner is forgiven and has salvation, he or she must still bear the marks of sin. How does the author use David's life as an example? Are there other Bible characters who also bore the marks of sin, even though they had been restored to God's favor?

Bible Investigation

1. In Romans 6:1–15 Paul tells us we can't continue in sin so that grace may abound. What reasoning does he use to show us the folly of this kind of thinking?
2. In Galatians 2:15–17 Paul says that when we seek to be justified in Christ, our sinfulness might become evident. However, that does not mean that Christ promotes sin. Do these verses apply to Chris-

tians in the church today? Does this have any relevance to those who reject the church because they say it's full of hypocrites? Does it bring hope to those of us who still struggle with sin in our lives?

Personal Application

Perhaps you are dealing with friends who think that God's scales are weighing their good deeds and bad deeds. How would you discuss this with them?

For Further Thought

In this day when so many Americans are deep in credit card debt, how great it is to know that the price for our salvation has been paid in full. How do we respond to this gift of salvation? Do other churches' teachings about penance as a way of proving our repentance ever seem to be appropriate or desirable as a response to our personal sin? Why or why not?

Starting Life over Again

In a recent poll, some Americans were asked whether they were satisfied with their lives or whether they would like to live life over again, or at least change it significantly. A large percentage responded that, given the opportunity, they would like to relive their lives. Yet that is impossible. Each person is born once and makes the best of the situation received, whether in terms of external circumstances or internal gifts and capacities. The Bible, however, speaks of a new beginning or "new birth." This new birth or regeneration is God's act of implanting a new spiritual dimension into a person's life and personality at the moment of conversion.

The Need for New Birth

Just as natural birth means that a new life has been created, so spiritual birth is proof of a new creation. In Ephesians 2:1, 5 Paul spoke of his readers having been "dead through trespasses and sins." He repeated this idea in Colossians 2:13.

The Bible also describes this condition of being dead as blindness. Jesus spoke of the Pharisees as blind leaders of the blind (Matt. 15:14); on another occasion he criticized their "blindness" (Matt. 23:16, 17, 19, 24, 26). Elsewhere in Scripture we read of a hardening or a lack of understanding (Rom. 11:25; Eph. 4:18) in unbelievers. It is viewed as Satan's work in John 12:40 (Jesus quoting Isa. 6:10) and 2 Corinthians 4:4. It is also described as a result of walking in darkness (1 John 2:11).

All these metaphors point to spiritual insensitivity. Before conversion people do not respond to spiritual things. All of us have probably been given a reflex test, in which the doctor raps our knees with a small mallet and our legs kick out in response. Where there is life, there will be response to an appropriate stimulus.

Several years ago I strained a muscle in my back. I went to the health service of the university where I was then studying. I made an appointment with an orthopedic surgeon. As I lay on the examining table, he jabbed a sharp instrument lightly into my thigh, and repeated the procedure with light stabs all the way down my leg. Then he did the same thing on the other leg. After inflicting each wound he asked, "Does that hurt?" In each case I repeated monotonously, "Yes." As I saw little red dots on my legs, he announced with satisfaction: "That's good. It's very good. That proves there is no paralysis." Where there is life, there will be response.

For the non-Christian, however, there is no sensitivity in spiritual matters. The truth of the gospel, the fact of his or her lostness and need of forgiveness, the glorious news of the grace of God—none of these evoke any significant response. While there are great differences among individuals, non-Christians are "spiritually dead." Sin is an anesthetic.

68

Thus, persons without Christ are incapable of fulfilling God's commands, or of changing themselves so that they might. In order to do what is right, they need three things:

1. Knowledge of what one should do
2. Desire to do what one should
3. Ability to do what one has decided to do

Anyone who sets out conscientiously to fulfill the Law of God faces disappointment and frustration. There is no neutrality here. Either we have difficulty perceiving the truth, or even if we see what is right we are not able to do what we see. *Original sin* is a very real fact. It works against our efforts to do the good. Romans 3:9–20 gives a vivid description of this flaw in unregenerate people.

In the face of this human weakness we can easily become pessimistic. When Jesus said it was harder for a rich man to enter the kingdom of heaven than for a camel to pass through the eye of a needle, the disciples were astonished and asked, "Then who can be saved?" Jesus indicated that what is impossible with humans is possible with God, for "with God all things are possible" (Matt. 19:23–26). The solution to a person's spiritual difficulty is not resolution or reformation, but transformation by God.

As a college student, I heard a theology professor describe his efforts at reformation during his pre-Christian days. He laid out his life into thirty areas, each involving some moral or spiritual issue. He assigned each of these to a different day of the month, then proceeded to master one area per day. On the first day he applied himself to patience, and perfectly practiced that virtue. The next day it was greed, and he was completely successful in overcoming that vice. Then he turned to mercy, and was as merciful a person as you could ever expect to find. So it continued throughout the month. On the last day, he conquered the final area, then looked back triumphantly over the chart of virtues and vices. Imagine his distress upon discovering that while he was improving his life by conquering lust and envy, the earlier vices of impatience and greed had returned to rage out of control.

Life is that way, isn't it? We may be successful in controlling one area of our lives for a short time, but we will never be able to manage all of them all of the time. Life is like a game two poor boys played during their childhood. Because money was scarce, organized activities requiring sports equipment were out of the question. Forced to improvise, these two lads devised a simple and inexpensive game. Each boy had a coffee can lid and several earthworms. He would take a worm, tie a knot in it, and place it on the lid. Then he would knot another worm the same way. The player who could keep the most worms knotted was the winner. I say "keep" because unfortunately the worm would not simply lie there, with the odd bulge in the middle of its body. It would begin to twist and squirm, thus effectively untying the knot. Human efforts at the moral life are like that. Everything keeps coming untied. We all need a new start.

The New Birth in Scripture

The witness to this special spiritual energizing is found throughout the Bible. God promised Israel that he would give them a new heart and a new spirit. He would take the stony heart out of their flesh and give them a heart of flesh. As a result they would walk in his statutes, keep his ordinances, and obey them; they would be his people, and he would be their God (Ezek. 11:19–21).

The New Testament term that would be literally translated "regeneration" occurs just twice. One of these usages, in Matthew 19:28, does not apply to the issue we are discussing. The other, in Titus 3:5, definitely does. It says, "He saved us, not on the basis of deeds which we have done in righteousness, but according to His mercy, by the washing of regeneration and renewing by the Holy Spirit." Although the term seldom occurs, the idea appears frequently.

The most extensive and familiar treatment of the subject is Jesus' conversation with Nicodemus. In John 3 Jesus twice spoke of being "born again." The expression he used can be translated either "born again (or anew)" or "born from above." Nicodemus's reaction suggests that he understood it in the first sense: "He cannot enter a second time into his mother's womb and be born, can he?" (v. 4). In the same passage Jesus also used the expression "born of the Spirit" three times (vv. 5–6, 8). He emphasized the contrast of spiritual birth with natural birth. One is by God's power; the other is by human action.

Other references speak of being "born of God" or "by the Word of God." One of these is John 1:12–13, which refers to "children of God" and describes believers as born, "not of blood, nor of the will of the flesh, nor of the will of man, but of God." John also wrote that "every one also who practices righteousness is born of Him" (1 John 2:29). "Whoever believes that Jesus is the Christ is born of God; and whoever loves the Father loves the child. . . . For whatever is born of God overcomes the world; and this is the victory that overcomes the world— our faith" (1 John 5:1, 4). James emphasized the activity of God and his use of the Word: "Of His will He brought us forth by the word of truth, so that we might be, as it were, the first fruits among His creatures"

(James 1:18). Peter referred to being "born anew" and related it especially to the resurrection: "Blessed be the God and Father of our Lord Jesus Christ, who according to His great mercy has caused us to be born again to a living hope through the resurrection of Jesus Christ from the dead. . . . You have been born again not of seed which is perishable but imperishable, that is, through the living and abiding word of God" (1 Peter 1:3, 23).

The concept is also expressed as "a new creation" or a transformation. Paul wrote, "Therefore if any man is in Christ, he is a new creature; the old things passed away, behold, new things have come" (2 Cor. 5:17).

In Titus 3:5 the term *regeneration* appears. The picture of renewal in the Holy Spirit is also present, and may be a parallel to the statement about regeneration: "He saved us, not on the basis of deeds which we have done in righteousness, but according to His mercy, by the washing of regeneration and renewing by the Holy Spirit."

In Ephesians, Paul spoke of this simply in terms of resurrection, or being made alive: "And you were dead in your trespasses and sins, in which you formerly walked according to the course of this world . . . even when we were dead in our transgressions, [God] made us alive together with Christ (by grace you have been saved), and raised us up with Him, and seated us with Him in the heavenly places, in Christ Jesus" (Eph. 2:1–2, 5–6).

Finally, there are Jesus' statements that he had come to give life. Some believed that he was inviting them to a limited way of life. In reality, just the opposite was true. Speaking of "his sheep," Jesus said, "The thief comes only to steal, and kill, and destroy; I came that they might have life, and might have it abundantly. . . . And I give eternal life to them, and they shall never perish" (John 10:10, 28). On another occasion he said, "It is the Spirit who gives life; the flesh profits nothing; the words that I have spoken to you are spirit and are life" (John 6:63).

The parable of the prodigal son also expresses the concept of coming to life. The father's final appeal to those present is, "This son of mine was dead, and has come to life again; he was lost, and has been found" (Luke 15:24). The same terms are used in his statement to the elder brother (v. 32).

The Difficulty of Understanding New Birth

Born again, born of God, a new creation, resurrection from the dead—all these phrases convey the idea that a change or transformation is produced when a person becomes a Christian. This is a difficult idea to grasp. Ultimately, it must remain incomprehensible. No explanation can ever give us complete understanding. Jesus himself encountered this difficulty in his conversation with Nicodemus. Nicodemus asked if the new birth was a physical process that required entering the mother's womb and literally being born a second time. Jesus replied that the new birth was not to be understood this way. The Spirit is like the wind. Jesus made a play on words here, since in both Hebrew and Greek "spirit" and "wind" are expressed by the same word.

One reason the new birth is so hard to understand is because it seems like a contradiction to our natural way of thinking. Usually we visualize ourselves as solving our own problems, reforming our own nature, becoming good enough. But sin is a matter of independence or self-sufficiency. The idea that God must radically transform us is foreign to our natural patterns or self-understanding.

Regeneration is also difficult to understand because it is not consciously experienced. We do not physically feel something happen the moment we are born again by God. Thus new birth cannot be specifically pinpointed in past experience. It is not a miracle, therefore, in the narrower meaning of that term, even though we sometimes speak of the "miracle of new birth."

Although the fact itself cannot be directly observed, the results may be discerned. As a new creature, the Christian thinks, feels, believes, chooses, and acts differently than before. This is the believer's evidence that God has accepted and regenerated him or her. So John wrote, "We know that we have passed out of death into life, because we love the brethren" (1 John 3:14).

Aspects of the New Birth

We cannot expect to understand completely this wonder of the new birth or make it easily understandable to others. But we can summarize the elements of this doctrine.

First, regeneration means adding a new dimension to the person's life or experience. One receives what may appropriately be termed *life.* While some think of the Christian life as narrow and restricting, the Bible pictures it as expanding the existence of the person. It is truly a new creation. It is not just an emphasis on tendencies already present. It is a unique energy, interest, and direction that cannot be accounted for except by rebirth.

Second, regeneration is a necessity. Humans need to please God, and God's approval only comes to them through the new birth. Jesus plainly told Nicodemus that apart from the new birth by the Spirit, one cannot enter the kingdom of God; indeed, one cannot even "see" the kingdom of God. It is the only acceptable admission ticket to the eternal presence of God.

The new birth is clearly a supernatural work. It is not a change that one can produce in oneself by mere resolution and effort. Nor is it a change that psychological methods can accomplish. This is clear from Jesus' contrast between "born of the Spirit" and "born of the flesh" (John 3:6). It is also contrasted with born "not of blood, nor of the will of the flesh, nor of the will of man" (John 1:13). Scripture affirms that only supernatural power will account for regeneration.

Rebirth is a gift provided by the work of Christ. We are declared righteous by virtue of his atonement. Similarly, our new life, pictured as resurrection, is based on our identification with his resurrection. The renewal of our lives depends on the resurrection of our Lord.

Regeneration is particularly the work of the Holy Spirit. This is indicated by Jesus' use of the expression "born of the Spirit" (John 3:6, 8) as virtually interchangeable with "born again" or "born from above." The Titus 3:5 reference to "renewal in the Holy Spirit" suggests the same.

Next, it gives new power for the battle with sin. As we noted earlier, regeneration is the injection of a completely new form of life, rather than merely an extension of the old. Nonetheless, it negates the effects of sin. Paul described the extent of the unbeliever's domination by sin's force (Eph. 2:1–5). He also emphasized the idea that this is now past, that a new order has come.

Finally, regeneration is just the beginning of a process, not its end. It is the implantation of a principle that grows and develops. The beginning assumes that the individual will continue to live in an appropriate way for a "new creature." Paul said, "For we are His workmanship, created in Christ Jesus for good works, which God prepared beforehand, that we should walk in them" (Eph. 2:10). Regeneration does not guarantee immediate perfection of Christian character. But it does activate a change that ultimately will result in a completely altered self.

Implications of the Doctrine

The concept of new birth speaks to four contemporary issues. The first is that humans are not basically good and that they need transformation. Lately, the idea of humanity's essential goodness has been revived. According to this view, if humans today are bad, it is not because of any flaw in their natures. Rather, it is a result of society's influence. If we remove or alter these influences, human goodness will reappear. From this view come the social, economic, and political programs intended to alter the existing order. Some attempt simply to modify it. Others, more radical in orientation, regard revolution as the means of change. The doctrine of regeneration, however, denies such a possibility. Humans need a major change of nature, and cannot bring about change on their own. The problem is not merely external and unimportant to human nature; it is internal and inherent.

Second, regeneration provides an answer to pessimism and despair. Many people take evil in this world very seriously. In some cases, as with the existentialists, this concern stems from a sense of the tragedy and emptiness of reality. Others despair because of the apparently fixed patterns of human personality. Because these patterns cannot be altered by any natural means, there is little hope for improvement. The Christian message addresses this sense of despair. Although it is pessimistic about innate human goodness, Christianity strongly affirms that human nature can be altered. New supernatural forces are available and each person can become a "new creature."

Third, regeneration implies the rejection of any type of nonrational fatalism. There are those who believe that human character and behavior are the result of forces neither conscious, intelligent, nor benevolent. One of these views is astrology. According to astrologers, what happens in life is governed by the positions of the heavenly bodies. The new science of sociobiology contends that genetic and evolutionary forces cause all behavior. But regeneration says that human identity and circumstances in life are really the work of God. God is the only Supreme Being and he is an intelligent and benevolent God. He wants each person to have the added spiritual dimension that only he can give.

Finally, regeneration teaches us that good is superior to evil. One of the great problems for Christian theology is the problem of evil: If God is completely good and loving and all powerful, how can there be such extensive evil in the world? Will good eventually overcome evil, or will it be the other way around? This large-scale problem is also seen in smaller dimensions in our lives. If God is all-powerful and good and loving, why are humans, created in his image and likeness, as evil as they are? Regeneration provides the solution to this problem. It establishes the redemptive work of God's grace in the human life and overcomes the force of sin, making us new creatures. And we are given reason to hope that the same will be true of the whole universe.

Study Guide

Key Questions

1. The author lists several ways in which the Bible describes our status before the new birth. What are they? Why is it helpful to have several descriptions?
2. The author suggests the following: (Fill in the blanks) Rebirth is a _____ provided by the work of Christ. It is the _____ of the Holy Spirit. Rebirth gives _____ for the battle with sin. Rebirth is the _____ of a process.

3. The doctrine of rebirth speaks to: (a) the idea that humans are not basically good; (b) despair; (c) non-rational fatalism (i.e., astrology, etc.); (d) the idea that good is not superior to evil. Do you hear any or all of these issues discussed by people you know? Which are the most common?

Bible Investigation

1. How does Ephesians 1:3 and Colossians 1:9–14 bear out any of the implications the author lists as results from the new birth?
2. What is the "good work" of Philippians 1:6 and how does it relate to this chapter?

Personal Application

1. As believers assess their own lives, do they clearly see the signs of regeneration or being born again? What are some of these signs?
2. Perhaps your experience of regeneration was very gradual, more like an educational process. Does this change the idea of a new birth experience? How? In what ways does this more gradual new-birth experience fit with the idea of being born again?

For Further Thought

Do you feel the term "born again" has been used derisively in our society? What is particularly good about the term as a description of regeneration? How might a Christian discuss this term so as to clarify all aspects of regeneration?

7

Christ and the Christian, Incorporated

As Jesus prepared to leave his disciples, he gave them his Great Commission and accompanied it with a promise: "I am with you always, even to the end of the age" (Matt. 28:20). So he is also with us, for the Scriptures speak of Christ and the Christian as joined by a special spiritual union. On the one hand, Paul described the believer as *in Christ*. He wrote, "If any man is in Christ, he is a new creature" (2 Cor. 5:17). On the other hand, we find that Christ is *in us*. Paul also wrote, "Christ in you, the hope of glory" (Col. 1:27). "I have been crucified with Christ; and it is no longer I who live, but Christ lives in me" (Gal. 2:20). If the Christian life is anything, it is a life lived in union with Jesus Christ.

This togetherness of the Christian and Christ is described in several ways:

1. Crucified with him   Galatians 2:20
2. Died with him   Colossians 2:20
3. Buried with him   Romans 6:4

4. Made alive with him	Ephesians 2:5
5. Raised with him	Colossians 3:1
6. Suffered with him	Romans 8:17
7. Glorified with him	Romans 8:17
8. Joint heirs with him	Romans 8:17

Inadequate Explanations of the Union

This is an impressive array of descriptions of union with Christ. But what does it mean? Is there some figure by which we can understand it? Several explanations have been offered. Let us note some inadequate or misleading explanations.

First, the Bible does not teach that we are part of God. It says God is present and active in all of creation, including the human race. Sometimes this idea is pressed so far, however, that the boundary between God and human beings is lost; no longer are God and I separate entities. Rather, we are both part of each other. I am God and he is I. This would mean that oneness with Christ is not really a matter of salvation because I am one with him by the mere fact of my existence. Union with God does not establish a new relationship; it expresses a natural condition. Many religions teach this concept. Under the influence of some of the Eastern religions, we may tend to think this way too. Note, however, that the Bible does not support such a position. According to the Bible, we are not a part of God, nor does a part of him naturally live in us.

Second, union with Christ is not a purely mystical one. Some believers emphasize devotion to Christ and concentrate on him so much that they think in terms of absorption in him, of being completely lost in him. In this view the believer virtually loses individual identity, ceasing to be aware of oneself, being caught up in Christ, as it were. This is similar to hypnosis, in which the person loses control of her own thoughts and will. She is like a ventriloquist's dummy, a mouthpiece, an empty shell. While Paul urged a Christian's deep commitment to Christ, he never suggested that that person lose his or her identity.

Third, union with Christ is not just a sympathetic union or a "meeting of the minds." This regards the oneness of the believer with Christ as an agreement, a common acceptance of ideals. Here the union between the believer and Christ is similar to that among Christians. It is like two friends who love the same things, have the same objectives, and understand one another. It is one person influencing the other or persuading the other to agree. It is a mere external influence, like two lines running parallel—perhaps very close to one another, but never really touching. The biblical picture, however, is a closer and stronger relationship than this.

Finally, we have the idea of sacramental union. In this view, the sacraments bring Christ and the believer together. Through the agency of a minister, the two are joined. The believer, in taking the Lord's Supper, eats Christ's flesh and drinks his blood, actually taking these into himself or herself. While this finds some superficial support in Scripture (John 6:53–54), it places a weight on these practices that the Bible does not. Furthermore, it introduces the idea of mediation of Christ's presence where the Bible depicts a direct relationship.

We may wonder about all these ideas. Each captures an element of truth, but not the whole truth. As we approach the full explanation of union with Christ, we must avoid falling into the trap of partial truth.

A Judicial Union

We may note first that union with Christ is a *judicial* union. Paul virtually identified the Christian and Christ in the great events of redemption: We were crucified with Christ, we died with him, we were made alive with him. When God considers the merit of the cross, he sees Christ and me together. Consequently, the benefits of Christ's atoning death are credited to me. When God examines my obligations before the Law, he does not see me alone. He sees both me and Jesus, and he says, "They are righteous." For all practical purposes, the cross creates a new legal standing, a special judicial or legal union.

A Vital Union

Beyond this, however, union with Christ is a *vital* union. Christ gave us more than external advice, encouragement, or an example. In a very real sense, he actually stimulates and energizes the sources of the spiritual life of the believer. He influences what the Christian thinks, feels, wills, does, and is. Jesus through the work of the Holy Spirit vitalizes the life of the Christian.

Jesus compared this union to the vine and the branches. He pictured himself as the vine and believers as branches. The branches, he said, are to bear fruit, and to that end the Heavenly Father trims and nurtures them. They are incapable of bearing fruit alone. Apart from the vine they produce nothing. But drawing life from the vine they can produce abundantly.

A number of other physical analogies of this vital union come to mind. One of these is mouth-to-mouth resuscitation, in which one person actually breathes for another. Another is the substitute heart. During cardiac surgery the patient's heart is bypassed and a mechanical heart performs the task of sending vital blood throughout the patient's body. Yet another is direct transfusion, in which blood is taken from one person's circulatory system and introduced directly into that of the other. In each of these examples, infusion of life comes through union with another.

There are also illustrations from the realm of psychology or of parapsychology. We are now aware of mental telepathy, the ability of one person to transmit thoughts from his or her mind to that of another.

Perhaps the closest analogy offered in Scripture is that of husband and wife. The Bible describes this relationship as "one flesh." In marriage there is an actual physical joining, but ideally there is also complete understanding and empathy between two people. Because of this fundamental agreement there can be encouragement and inspiration surpassing even the close relationship of friends. That is why Paul used marriage to illustrate the relationship between Christ and the church.

We need to note, however, that in the union of Christ and the Christian neither party loses individual identity. This sets Christianity apart from Hinduism. There is no absorption, no blending of egos. The union is of two individuals.

Weddings sometimes include a candle-lighting ceremony. As the service begins, two lighted candles stand on each side of the altar. At some point in the service the bride and groom each take one of the lighted candles and together light a single, unlighted candle. Each extinguishes his or her candle. Only one new light burns on.

I am always a bit uneasy at such weddings. The candle ceremony suggests that there is to be no continuing individuality. The two persons cease to be, in favor of one new unipersonality. In the light of the true nature of the marriage relationship, it would be more appropriate to keep the two original candles burning along with the one newly lighted candle. This would symbolize a genuine unity of two differing individuals.

Christ and the Christian, Incorporated   83

Similarly, in our relationship with Christ we do not cease to be. If we did, if we were merely absorbed into him, then all diversity among Christians—which Paul applauds in the church—would presumably cease. Thankfully, in Christ we still retain our own personalities.

Results of the Union

Because of our union with Christ, we can enjoy several experiences that are shared only with other true believers. Let's look at these results of our unity with Christ.

Victory. As we have seen, the Bible teaches that salvation in and through Jesus Christ is experienced by the believer. The first result of this union is victory over sin and the flesh. Paul indicated that we have died with Christ (Rom. 6:1–11). It is almost as if Paul saw us at the cross with our hands and feet laid upon his, and the nails driven through ours along with his. Our "old self" was crucified, our sinful flesh destroyed (v. 6). We are freed, therefore, from the slavery of sin (v. 7). We can claim victory over the domination of sin.

Christians must be aware of this victory and continually base their lives and experiences on it. At midnight, May 8, 1945, World War II officially ended in Europe. But between the signing of the armistice and its becoming effective, fighting continued in some isolated pockets where communication was poor. Men continued to fight and some even died in a war that was already over.

Similarly, there are persons named in wills who have never received their inheritances because they do not know of their good fortune. No one is able to locate them. So it is with the person who has never realized that in Christ we are dead to sin.

Justification. A second significant fact about our union with Christ is the judicial reality we have already noted. In marriage, the assets and liabilities of the two partners are ordinarily merged. So here the spiritual assets and liabilities of Christ and the Christian are brought together. A new entity emerges, "Jesus Christ and John Doe, incorporated." The Christian need no longer bear the weight of his or her own guilt. This was assumed by Christ. Similarly, the Christian's standing with God is not dependent on the Christian's goodness. The perfect righteousness of Christ has become the believer's.

Some critics of the substitutionary atonement charge that it is improper for one person to be executed for another, or for a person to be treated as righteous when he or she really is not. The answer to this criticism lies in the unique oneness of Christ and the Christian. As Christ and the believer were crucified and condemned together, they also are resurrected and justified together.

Living with Christ. The Christian also finds encouragement and challenge in knowing that the Christian life is lived together with Christ. When Jesus sent his disciples into the world (Matt. 28:19–20), he did not send them away alone. He assured them that he would always be with them, even to the end of the age. This promise looked forward to the coming of the Holy Spirit, through whom Jesus is spiritually present with his people.

The special ministry of the Holy Spirit is taught in Jesus' message in John 15. He described his relationship to the disciples as that of the vine to the branches. Their spiritual vitality, he indicated, came from him. As they lived in him, they would produce fruit to honor him.

This suggests that Christ's strength is continually available to the believer. That is why Paul wrote, "I can do all things through Him who strengthens me" (Phil. 4:13). In Christ even weakness becomes strength. When Paul was afflicted by his "thorn in the flesh"—in all probability some physical ailment—he prayed and asked three times that it be taken from him. Each time God denied the request. The denial was accompanied, however, by the assurance that he would be given sufficient grace to bear this trial. The Lord's response was: "My grace is sufficient for you, for power is perfected in weakness" (2 Cor. 12:9). Paul found that handicaps can have a positive effect. He said, "I will rather boast about my weaknesses, that the power of Christ may dwell in me . . . for when I am weak, then I am strong" (vv. 9–10).

Paul apparently had thought he was strong enough to cope with his problems. He did not really feel it necessary to draw on Christ's power. The thorn in the flesh, however, made him painfully aware of his own weakness. He was forced to depend on the Lord's strength. And he found that besides his own slight strength, he had Christ's abundant power. Thus his weakness revealed his true spiritual strength. We might paraphrase Paul's statement: "When I am weak then *we* are strong."

Thus, Christians need not despair because of their limitations. They are not alone. When David faced Goliath in battle, the conflict seemed unfair. It was, but not in the way it appeared. Goliath was large (almost ten feet tall) and strong. But Goliath was alone. David was small, but he was not alone. The real conflict was Goliath versus the team of David and Jehovah, and that was really no competition. In the context of New Testament salvation, the same is true for us.

Christians are simply channels of God's grace and power. There is no basis for pride or boasting. Jesus said, "Apart from Me you can do nothing" (John 15:5). Christians always need to be aware of this. We should be humbly grateful that Christ has chosen to use us, and be ready to give Christ the credit, rather than taking all the honor for ourselves.

If we fail in this, we may be like the woodpecker that landed on a telephone pole and reared back to make his first peck. At the exact second his beak contacted the wood a lightning bolt struck the pole. It was shattered by the blast, and the woodpecker was knocked unconscious. When he finally regained consciousness, he found himself lying on his back in the midst of what resembled the remains of a toothpick factory. Surveying the wreckage about him he exclaimed, "I didn't know I had it in me!" We need to realize that spiritual results may come to us, but it is Christ who is the power of God for our salvation.

Suffering with Christ. A fourth major dimension of the oneness of the Savior and the saved one is suffering together. The disciples who wanted the privilege of sitting at the right and left hands of Christ in the kingdom were told that they would drink the cup that he would drink and be baptized with his baptism (Mark 10:39). John 15:20 shows that Jesus meant that the same suffering soon to come upon him would be their experience also. On the eve of his crucifixion Jesus told his disciples that they would also be exposed to the same treatment he was about to receive. He said: "Remember the word that I said to you, 'A slave is not greater than his master.' If they persecuted Me, they will also persecute you" (John 15:20). If we can trust early Christian tradition, Jesus' forecast came true. Early Christian reports tell us that each of the eleven remaining disciples of the Lord died a martyr's death.

We know for sure that Paul aspired to this oneness with Christ. He wrote: "That I may know . . . the fellowship of His sufferings, being conformed to His death" (Phil. 3:10). Such suffering, said Peter, is a cause for rejoicing—if it is suffering we undergo because of bearing the name of Christ (1 Peter 4:14). At the same time, each of us must make certain that our suffering is a result of our identification with Christ. Peter pointed out (v. 15) that there is no virtue in suffering, if that suffering is because of our own wrongdoing. Sometimes Christians assume that the difficulties they find in their relationships with others are due to their Christian convictions. In fact, religious convictions may have nothing to do with it. Real suffering for the sake of Christ need not trouble us. It will come as a normal consequence of living a genuine Christian life.

Ruling with Christ. The final dimension of union with Christ is the believer's glorification. All in Christ will rule with him. Time and again in Scripture reigning with Christ is linked with suffering with Christ. Suffering together results in ruling together. Paul said: "We are children of God, and if children, heirs also, heirs of God and fellow-heirs with Christ, if indeed we suffer with Him in order that we may also be glorified with Him" (Rom. 8:16–17). In 2 Timothy 2:12, he added, "If we endure, we shall also reign with Him." Peter said, "But to the degree that you share the sufferings of Christ keep on rejoicing; so that also at the revelation of His glory you may rejoice with exultation" (1 Peter 4:13). And, finally, Jesus told his disciples, "You are those who have stood by Me in My trials. . . . I grant you that you may eat and drink at My table in My kingdom, and you will sit on thrones judging the twelve tribes of Israel" (Luke 22:28–30).

This means that if we go with Jesus anywhere he asks us to go, he will take us with him wherever he goes. Our close identification with Christ, beautifully symbolized by baptism (Rom. 6:1–11), is the truth expressed in that song that was often sung during baptisms in many evangelical churches:

I'll go with Him through the judgment,
I'll go with Him through the judgment,
I'll go with Him through the judgment,
I'll go with Him, with Him, all the way.

He will give me grace and glory,
He will give me grace and glory,
He will give me grace and glory,
And go with me, with me, all the way.

Study Guide

Key Questions

1. Paul often talked about Christians being "in Christ." How do we participate with Christ in his crucifixion (Gal. 2:20), his death (Col. 2:20), his burial (Rom. 6:4), his resurrection (Eph. 2:5; Col. 3:1), his suffering (Rom. 8:17), and his glorification (Rom. 8:17)?
2. Victory over sin is one of the results of union with Christ. See Romans 6:1–11. How does the author's use of the ending of hostilities in Europe on May 8, 1945, relate to a Christian's claim to victory over sin?

Bible Investigation

1. Read 2 Corinthians 12:9–10. How does this chapter's title, "Christ and the Christian, Incorporated," relate to these verses?
2. In Romans 6:1–11, Paul speaks of our participation in Christ's death and resurrection. In verses 11–14, Paul admonishes us not to give parts of our body over to sin as instruments of wickedness. What might giving our mind to sin as an instrument of wickedness entail?

Personal Application

1. Have you ever been grateful that you are absolutely unique as one of God's creatures? Rather than bemoaning our lack of specific gifts from God, what

attitude should we have regarding any gift we have? What would the world be like if we all had been given the same gifts? How about the church?

2. A young girl related that her baptism experience meant to her that she would like to follow the Lord to the mission field somewhere. Is her experience unique or is it the natural outflow of following Jesus? What does your baptismal experience mean to you?

For Further Thought

Consider the ideas of Hinduism, pantheism, and New Age philosophies as they relate to our oneness with God. Think about the distinction of Christians in Christianity as exemplified in Paul's description of the church as a physical body in 1 Corinthians 12.

You're in the Family Now

Much teaching about salvation places it in a legal context. This is appropriate, for salvation involves such judicial concepts as guilt, remission, and pardon. But salvation is also a warm, personal matter.

One beautiful expression of salvation is given in the idea of adoption. In Greek the term means literally "placing as sons." The Bible says, "As many as received Him, to them He gave the right to become children of God, even to those who believe in His name" (John 1:12). This acceptance was part of God's eternal plan: "He predestined us to adoption as sons through Jesus Christ to Himself, according to the kind intention of His will" (Eph. 1:5). And for this reason Christ came into the world: "But when the fulness of the time came, God sent forth His Son, born of a woman, born under the law, in order that He might redeem those who were under the Law, that we might receive the adoption as sons" (Gal. 4:4–5). If justification is primarily a legal and somewhat negative idea, then adoption is its personal and positive counterpart.

Adoption, however, is not the original relationship God intended between himself and the Christian. It is, as it were, *re*-adoption, for it represents the restoration of the original relationship that has been broken. In one sense the Bible presents God as the Father of all people. He created all and continues to bestow life on all, whether they believe in him or not. Paul made this point in his speech on Mars Hill (Acts 17:25–29) and the idea is implied in both Hebrews 12:9 and James 1:18. Because of sin, however, we are estranged and rebellious children. So adoption is God's way of restoring the relationship he originally intended for us. This relationship has several important aspects.

Adoption and Forgiveness

First, adoption involves forgiveness beyond the remission of penalty. We may be acquitted by a court or pay the penalty, but the offended person may still feel bitterness or resentment toward us. One term used of God's forgiveness emphasizes the gracious, favorable disposition he has toward us. Thus Paul urged his readers to "be kind to one another, tender-hearted, forgiving each other, just as God in Christ also has forgiven you" (Eph. 4:32). Forgiveness means the removal of that ill will that once marred our relationship because of sin.

What a wonderful sense of relief it is to experience God's forgiveness! And, conversely, what anguish to be unable to obtain that forgiveness. I realized this forcefully as a young boy when I became angry and resentful toward my sister for some reason. I wanted to get even with her by hurting her. Since she was five years older than I, a direct assault did not seem wise.

I looked for a way to get revenge and found it. I saw her bicycle with its inflated balloon tires. Unobserved, I pounded a large nail into the front tire, then pulled out the nail and watched triumphantly as the tire went flat. My joy was complete. I had avenged myself upon my tormentor.

When Eileen discovered the flat tire, I faked my sympathy, but inwardly I rejoiced at her predicament. But later I began to feel sorry for what I had done. I confessed my crime to my parents and my sister. But they didn't believe me. I don't think it was because they couldn't believe I would do such a thing as much as the fact that they were surprised that I would confess such a crime. They would not take me seriously, and as a result I was miserable. I was free from punishment. But I wanted something more—positive forgiveness and acceptance. When I finally succeeded in persuading my sister and parents and obtaining their forgiveness, I felt a profound sense of relief. Paul emphasized this when he wrote, "Therefore, having been justified by faith, we have peace with God through our Lord Jesus Christ" (Rom. 5:1).

Adoption and Reconciliation

Adoption also involves reconciliation. Christ's death served to reconcile us to God by paying the debt we owed to God. The effect of sin is somewhat like the effect of a quarrel between two people. Even after God's side of the quarrel is resolved, resentment from the human side remains. People fear God, and therefore, as a defense mechanism, raise opposition and accusations against God. Furthermore, we usually expect God to send only good into our lives and when pain or sorrow or disappointment comes, we blame God for it. So humans need to have this fear and animosity toward God removed.

Christ died to bring us back to God. While his sacrifice was primarily for the Father, enabling him to accept us, it also has a secondary effect on us. In Jesus' death we have a beautiful demonstration of the quality and extent of the Father's love for us. It's like two friends who are quarreling as they walk along a riverbank. In the midst of their argument, one of them slips and falls into the stream. "I can't swim," he calls out. "I'm going to drown." Without hesitation the other person dives into the water and pulls his friend safely to shore. It is unlikely that the rescued person would immediately resume the argument. Instead, he would be impressed by the demonstration of his friend's love, who risked his own life to rescue him. This would overwhelm any irritation about the petty quarrel they had just had.

So it is with God. Giving his Son to save us is a profound demonstration of the extent of his love. Paul wrote, "But God demonstrates His own love toward us, in that while we were yet sinners, Christ died for us" (Rom. 5:8). John put it this way: "In this is love, not that we loved God, but that He loved us and sent His Son to be the propitiation for our sins" (1 John 4:10). Paul wrote that God was in Christ reconciling the world to himself (2 Cor. 5:16–21). His appeal came from this: "We beg you on behalf of Christ, be reconciled to God" (v. 20).

Adoption and Liberty

Along with Paul's figure of adoption is the idea of coming to maturity and to the *liberty* it brings. This thought is particularly prominent in Galatians 4, where the heir, under guardians and trustees as a child, is contrasted with the son, who has come of age. In Romans 8:14–15, the contrast is between the spirit of adoption as sons and the spirit of bondage as slaves. In each case Paul referred to freedom from the Law. In former days his readers were in bondage to the elemental spirits (Gal. 4:9). They were keepers of days and seasons. But salvation by grace made them sons and delivered them from their attempts to keep the Law. So now, he argued, they lived and walked in the Spirit instead.

Paul was teaching that the believer's salvation and growth do not depend on keeping certain laws. The church at Galatia faced this same problem. Some teachers there announced that observing the Jewish Law, specifically circumcision, was necessary for salvation. Paul sternly denounced this. Believers, he argued, were no longer under the Law. They were now sons and heirs. The Law had never had the power to declare righteousness or to justify. It served only to condemn because no one was capable of fulfilling it completely (Gal. 3:10–11). Since Christ fulfilled the Law for us, we are delivered from the necessity and the impossibility of having to fulfill its demands.

Adoption and Obedience

This does not mean, however, that obedience is no longer expected of us. We do not obey God as slaves, but as sons. Paul pointed out that Christian freedom was not an invitation to gratify the flesh (Gal. 5:13–16). He urged the Galatians to walk in the Spirit, and through love to serve one another. He gave them certain instructions and expected obedience. By the same measure, Jesus told his disciples that they were no longer slaves but friends (John 15:15). He said, "You are My friends, if you do what I command you" (John 15:14); "If you love Me, you will keep My commandments" (John 14:15); and "He who has My commandments and keeps them, he it is who loves Me" (John 14:21). Freedom, then, does not mean that we disregard the Father's will or disobey his commands, but that we do not do them slavishly.

Legalism is not so much a matter of *what* is done, as *how* it is done. There is a difference between "rule-ism" or "law-ism" and legalism. Until my teenage years, we did not have electricity on our farm. Water was pumped by a windmill, the radio ran off an electrical storage battery charged by a windcharger, and food was kept cool in an icebox. Ice cream was an unusual treat. Lacking a freezer, we had to eat it as soon as our parents returned from the grocery store. As so often happens when children are involved, disputes broke out over who got the biggest portion.

On one occasion, I took a ruler and laid it against the edge of the brick of ice cream and measured it into five exactly equal portions. I marked the divisions on the top and bottom edge of each of the two sides. Then I carefully cut the block of ice cream into five pieces, nearly exactly equal in size. It is not legalistic to say that each person should have an equal amount. That is simple fairness. But to divide with micrometric exactness so that not one may have even a shade more or less, and then feel smug satisfaction that justice has been executed—that is legalistic.

Christians who realize the truth of adoption will seek to do the Father's will, and will strive to please him because they love the Father. They are no longer slaves who obey out of fear of the consequences. While we seek to do God's will as fully as possible, we need not dread the consequences should we fail.

Adoption and Fatherly Care

Adoption means there is an intimacy and warmth to the relationship between the believer and God. Paul spoke of how we have received the spirit of sonship rather than slavery (Rom. 8:15; Gal. 4:6). This causes us to cry, "Abba! Father!" The word transliterated here from the Aramaic is an intimate word for father. It is similar to the child's "dad," "daddy," or "papa." It is the term of endearment a small child uses in addressing his or her beloved father. Paul pointed out that when we address God this way, the Spirit is thereby witnessing to the fact that we are now children of God, not merely slaves. Because we are children, we can expect certain kinds of care and provision from God. We are now heirs and fellow heirs with Christ (Rom. 8:17). When Paul wrote to the Philippians, "And my God shall supply all your needs according to His riches in glory in Christ Jesus" (4:19), he was applying this truth. What the Father has is ours. One day we will receive all that is ours. For now, however, we may call on him to supply all our needs. We are not strangers. He is our "dada." A child cannot expect special provision or protection from an adult stranger. An adult will feel no special responsibility to just any child. But when the child involved is his own, he will be deeply concerned for the child's welfare.

This gives us confidence and boldness in our prayers. We all feel greater freedom in bringing our concerns to someone who knows and loves us. Thus Jesus reminded us that we pray to our Father who is in heaven (Matt. 6:9). He was urging us to bear in mind the God to whom we pray and what he is like. He is a loving, concerned, benevolent Father.

Not only does this remove the timidity and fear we might have in approaching a stranger, but it builds our confidence that the God who will answer is wise, good, and powerful. Thus Jesus taught that children don't have to be afraid to ask their Heavenly Father for things. A human father will not give his child a serpent when he asks for a fish, or a scorpion when he requests an egg. God in his wisdom knows better than we do what is really good for us. He sometimes withholds what we ask for, protecting us against our own desires and foolishnesses (Luke 11:11–13).

In many ways adoption is closely linked to the Holy Spirit's coming and living in the believers. The children of God are no longer led by the Law or dominated by the flesh. Rather, they are now led by the Spirit of God (Rom. 8:14). He is the Father's means of guiding the life of the believer. He produces the fruit of the Spirit.

Members of human families usually have noticeable resemblances. For example, children often have facial features like their parents'. Or they may have a similar stance or gait. Sometimes the voices of parent and child are virtually indistinguishable, particularly over the telephone. Or they may share expressions of speech. Similarly, the Holy Spirit is the "spiritual genetic factor," producing the family characteristics known as "the fruit of the Spirit" (Gal. 5:22–23).

Adoption and Discipline

Part of a child's rearing is parental discipline or chastening. Children usually don't consider this a benefit or a blessing, but that is the way Scripture pictures it. The writer of the letter to the Hebrews develops this theme at some length (12:5–11). Sometimes, believers are distressed at the unpleasant experiences that come into their lives. They find them hard to take (v. 3). But these may be a cause for rejoicing, if they are actually the Father's means of disciplining his children. The father who disciplines does so because he loves his children. Indulgence and permissiveness are really not signs of love. They are more likely signs of indifference. Love, however, involves concern and action for the child's welfare. If we are not disciplined, we are not really children but illegitimate offspring.

Christians realize and accept this truth. Rather than rebelling against the Father for permitting unpleasant experiences to come into their lives, they rejoice in these experiences. This is not because they enjoy them. Rather, Christians realize that these disciplinary activities are maturing and perfecting them, and that is their ultimate desire. Also, the presence of such discipline proves that the Father genuinely loves them.

This paternal love is not indulgent; nor is it overprotective. Sometimes a parent who loves her child must restrain herself when she sees her child doing something that will result in pain and disappointment. The parent is tempted to rush in and solve the child's problem for him. To do this, however, deprives the child of the opportunity to learn to cope with life. Thus, sometimes God allows things to happen that he does not send, simply because the child must learn from these experiences.

A parent's love for the adopted child is also patient. This is part of the child's security. She need not fear that one slip will cause the Father to disown her. God called Israel his son: "Israel is My firstborn son" (Exod. 4:22; cf. Deut. 14:1; 32:6; Jer. 31:9; Hos. 11:1). Yet, think of the patience God had with Israel. Once Israel even wanted to return to Egypt, out of which God had called them. The people of Israel disobeyed God's commands, rejected his prophets, and worshiped false gods. Yet God continued to exercise his "steadfast love." In the New Testament, the same was true. God kept seeking and drawing the indifferent and even rebellious ones to himself.

The prodigal son's father illustrates this beautifully. He never stopped loving his son. Although the son gave no indication when he left that he would ever return, the father continued to watch and wait. When the son returned, he realized he was no longer worthy of his father's love and didn't deserve to be treated as a son. He had taken all that was rightfully his and had squandered it. Now he wanted to be treated as a mere hired hand. The father, however, would have none of this. He insisted on celebrating and giving to the boy the symbols of his status as a son. He had been dead but was alive again.

Adoption and the Father's Good Will

In an earlier chapter, we noted that the expression "just as if I had never sinned" is not completely adequate. God literally carries nothing over from our past sin. Restoration is really complete. No suspicion or guilt remains. It is as if the incident had never occurred.

There is a vast difference between mere pardon and positive good will. A person may be tried and convicted of a crime, and sentenced to prison. When that sentence is served, the criminal is "square with the law." He cannot be held in prison or returned to it (unless he commits another offense). That, however, gives him no positive benefits. He may get a new suit of clothes, a handshake, and a slap on the back from the warden. But that hardly guarantees him success and happiness in life. He may find people who, if they discover his criminal record, will not employ him, or are reluctant to have him live near them or associate with them. The law can make him free from further punishment, but it cannot guarantee him freedom from people's prejudices. Fear and suspicion that he may commit the same crime again create an unwillingness to trust him.

Sometimes we hear the expression, "I forgive, but I can't forget." This means that although we will take no formal action against the other person, we still have some distrust. We realize that this person has failed in the past and that he or she is capable of failing again.

The doctrine of adoption means much more than that. It is a declaration of God's positive attitude toward us. God does not merely say, "You've done wrong in the past, and are now guiltless. But I will be here, watching your every action because I expect you to do something like that again." Adoption means that God says, "You have done wrong in the past, but are now righteous. I know, however, that there is a danger that you may fail again, but I'm here to take your hand and help you." The Judge of justification has become the Father of adoption.

Study Guide

Key Questions

1. If the doctrine of justification is a legal aspect of personal salvation, then its personal counterpart is adoption, according to the author. Which of these two parts do we think about most often in the Christian life? Why? Why should both aspects be part of our awareness of what God has done for us?
2. The author suggests that legalism is not so much a matter of what is done, as how it is done. What does he mean by this? Can you think of a New Testament Bible character whose life exemplifies this? Why is this important?
3. Because God the Father has adopted us, what might we expect out of this relationship (Rom. 8:15–17; Gal. 4:6; Phil. 4:19)?

Bible Investigation

1. In Acts 17:25–29, Paul refers to all humankind as God's offspring. How does this relate to Genesis 1:27? Can you think of other verses that refer to us as family members?
2. The story of the prodigal son mirrors the family relationship children of God have with their Heavenly Father. List some of the characteristics of this relationship, beyond the most obvious forgiveness factor.
3. In Galatians 4:4–7 Paul speaks of sonship versus slaveship. We are allowed to be sons (or children)

because of Jesus' work on the cross. What are some of the blessings that accompany the parent–child relationship that aren't in the master–slave relationship?

Personal Application

1. Adopted children are often reminded that they are very special to their parents because they were chosen. How does this idea carry over to our adoption by God the Father?
2. Family members are often quite similar. In our Christian family, what should some of the resemblances be (Gal. 5:22–23)? Specifically, what do you look for first in other Christians?

For Further Thought

Along with family love comes parental discipline (Heb. 12:7–11). Does hardship that comes our way always produce a harvest of righteousness and peace that's mentioned in verse 11? What is a harvest of righteousness and peace? What examples in your life or others' lives exemplify this?

9

There's a New You Coming

Have you ever seen a new building that has never been occupied, an automobile never driven, or an admission ticket never used? There is something sad about these things. They represent unfulfilled potential. So would our salvation if it meant merely conversion, justification, and generation. These are only the beginnings of God's work in us.

Sanctification is the continuation of that divine activity. It is described in numerous ways in Scripture, but one of the most emphatic promises is found in Philippians 1:6. "For I am confident of this very thing, that He who began a good work in you will perfect it until the day of Christ Jesus." The new life begun in regeneration is continued and developed toward completion. The babe in Jesus Christ continues to grow and mature. We call this growth process sanctification.

Two Meanings of Sanctification

The word *sanctification* is the translation of a Greek word meaning "to make holy." Sanctification as a term is used two ways. First, it refers to *positional sanctification.* This refers to something or someone who has been set apart, or designated as specifically belonging to the Lord. In the Old Testament, various objects, sacrificial animals, and special persons (such as priests and Levites) were designated as God's special property. They were "holy unto their God" (cf. Lev. 21:6 KJV). In this sense, all believers can be referred to as "saints" or "holy ones." They are God's property, to be used by him, to serve him and accomplish his purposes. The frequent references to "saints" in Paul's epistles and elsewhere have this meaning in view.

Second, it refers to *progressive sanctification*—the Spirit of God's continuous working in the life of believers. He changes the believers' character so that they will experience more and more of what they really are in Christ. Step by step the children of God grow in the likeness of the Lord.

Sanctification and Justification

It is important to contrast sanctification and justification. While these are two parts of the doctrine of salvation, they emphasize different aspects of the doctrine and should not be confused. There are a number of significant points of difference.

Justification is an instantaneous act of God. It happens in the moment of conversion. But sanctification is a progressive work, extending over a long period of time, indeed, over the remainder of the believer's life.

Justification is an all-or-nothing matter. One is either justified or not. No one is 50 percent justified, 20 percent justified, or more justified than anyone else. Justification is complete and the same in all believers. Sanctification, on the other hand, being a progressive matter, varies in degree from one Christian to another.

Justification changes a person's relationship with God. Sanctification, however, involves a change in the character of the individual, whose relational status has already been changed.

Justification is objective—it is done externally for us. Sanctification, by contrast, is internal. It is what God does within our lives. We may call it subjective, but we should remember that it is not dependent on our feelings. It is a work done to us by someone from without.

Sanctification as Divinely Produced Christlikeness

Sanctification is more than mere *reform.* It is something more complete, thorough, and crucial. It is a supernatural work. It is supernatural because human nature can neither produce it nor explain it. It is more than education, counsel, or behavior modification. No human effort can produce its results. The Holy Spirit might utilize human beings to achieve his purposes, but humans cannot produce the spiritual change of sanctification by their own clever efforts.

Sanctification is also supernatural because it is a special work of the Holy Spirit. It is not merely his common, everyday working, sometimes referred to as general providence or common grace. It does not occur automatically or at a fixed rate.

Scripture often underscores this supernatural character of sanctification. Some references indicate that God is its Author. One of these is 1 Thessalonians 5:23, "May the God of peace Himself sanctify you entirely." Similar statements are found in Hebrews 13:20–21, Titus 2:14, and Ephesians 5:26. Other references instruct us to pray for the grace of God. Paul wrote about "Him who is able to do exceeding abundantly above all that we ask or think, according to the power that works within us" (Eph. 3:20).

The purpose of this special work of God is that we should become like Jesus Christ, God's Son. In Romans 8:29 Paul described God's great plan: "For whom He foreknew, He also predestined to become conformed to the image of His Son, that He might be the Firstborn among many brethren."

This is a genuine likeness to Christ, not just a superficial resemblance. There are two words for "form" in the Greek language. One word refers to a mere external appearance, a facade. A college friend tested the beauty of the attractive young women he dated with a "trial by water." He would take a girl swimming, push her head under water, and hold it there a few seconds; then he would pull her out and see what was left. Beauty that washes away, he felt, isn't even skin deep.

There is a spirituality like that, external and artificial. If Paul had used the first word for form, he would have meant, "that we might seem to be like Jesus." Instead, he used a word that means an outward manifestation of the real nature of something. It does not merely resemble the other; it is of the same nature. This means that in sanctification we are actually taking on the character of Jesus Christ. We are not assuming his divine nature. That will never be the case. But we are acquiring the same love, patience, faithfulness, dedication, and other qualities Jesus had. So Paul spoke of Jesus as the firstborn of many brethren. There are to be, in a sense, many Christs, not just one. And this is no afterthought on God's part. He has always had this plan for us, and therefore brought us into being.

We do not gain this likeness to Christ apart from him. The word "conformed" suggests a living attachment to him. We noted this in the chapter dealing with our union with Christ. It is a key factor in this aspect of our salvation as well.

In the process of making us like Jesus Christ, God uses

everything. Paul wrote, "We know that God causes all things to work together for good to those who love God, to those who are called according to His purpose" (Rom. 8:28). Many Christians know this verse. Next to Romans 3:23 and 6:23, it is probably the best known and most frequently quoted verse from the Book of Romans. We find comfort in knowing that God is working for our best interest through all circumstances. This knowledge of God's work in our lives does more than give us a sense of security. It produces the likeness of Christ in us (Rom. 8:29).

We usually think of God as using the obviously "good" things, such as the church, the Bible, and added blessings to draw us closer to him. But the verse suggests that "all things"—both the obviously good and the seemingly evil—are employed by God. Not everything coming our way may be caused or sent by God, but he does use everything. Sometimes God even uses suffering to purify our lives and remove flaws.

It isn't that suffering is God's purpose for us. Likeness to Christ is his intention. He doesn't want to hurt us, but sometimes health comes only through pain. God is like a surgeon who must remove a diseased organ or a foreign object from a patient's body. The surgeon cuts and injures otherwise healthy tissue, in the process inflicting pain. But the surgeon does not inflict pain because she wants the patient to suffer, but because she wants to bring health. It is the process that is painful. The patient, knowing the doctor's good intention, does not resent the knife. He does not enjoy the pain, but he endures it, and even rejoices because he knows the pain will improve his health, which is quite different from the pain of illness.

Peter said, "In this you greatly rejoice, even though now for a little while, if necessary, you have been distressed by various trials, that the proof of your faith, being more precious than gold which is perishable even though tested by fire, may be found to result in praise and glory and honor at the revelation of Jesus Christ" (1 Peter 1:6–7). James expressed something similar when he wrote, "Consider it all joy, my brethren, when you encounter various trials, knowing that the testing of your faith produces endurance. And let endurance have its perfect result, that you may be perfect and complete, lacking in nothing" (James 1:2–4).

Sanctification as the Holy Spirit's Working

Sanctification is particularly the work of the Holy Spirit in us. In Galatians 5, Paul spoke of walking by the Spirit (v. 16) and living by the Spirit (v. 25). He contrasted this with gratifying the desires of the flesh (v. 16). He also listed virtues he called the "fruit of the Spirit" (vv. 22–23) and contrasted these with the "works of the flesh" (vv. 19–21). The fruit of the Spirit in those he indwells includes love, joy, peace, patience, kindness, goodness, faithfulness, gentleness, and self-control. These are the evidences of the Spirit's work within us.

It may seem strange that "fruit" is singular here, when a whole list of qualities is enumerated. Paul probably intended to show that the Spirit produces these collectively rather than as isolated entities. Some people seem to have certain qualities "naturally." There are people who are by nature gentle. Others seem to be unusually patient. We might wonder, therefore, whether spirituality may be possible apart from God's special working, since some of these people make no claim to be Christians. The answer, however, lies not in a single quality but in the combination. The cluster is the work of the Holy Spirit alone. So, for example, the naturally joyous person may not be self-controlled. When the Spirit is active, however, the well-rounded Christian character is present.

These qualities prove the Holy Spirit's presence and activity. We can discern his leading when we find his fruit: joy, love, self-control, and the other qualities. Jealousy, anger, or dissension, on the other hand, shows that the flesh is motivating us. The Holy Spirit does not produce such feelings. The flesh generates the works of the flesh; the Spirit gives the fruit of the Spirit.

The Christian's Role in Sanctification

From the foregoing, we might infer that the Christian is totally passive in sanctification. Scripture, however, suggests otherwise. In Romans 8:28, Paul said, "God causes all things to work together for good to those who love God." Literally, the text says, "God *with-works.*" Paul taught much the same thing in Philippians 2:12–13. Speaking of the process of salvation or what we would call sanctification, he wrote, "Work out your salvation with fear and trembling; for it is God who is at work in you, both to will and to work for His good pleasure." The action of God and the action of the human are not mutually exclusive. On the contrary, they are interrelated.

Certainly the Apostle gave no basis for inactivity or idleness. We may not simply sit around, saying, "I will not try to change myself or improve my Christian character. When God is ready to make me a more mature Christian, he will do it." Nor, on the other hand, is there any place for pride, so that we might say, "See what a fine Christian I have made of myself." Sanctification is neither all of God nor all of us. It is not even that each of us does a part, supplementing the work of the other. Rather, in all we do God is there, penetrating and motivating and spurring both our will and our action.

Scripture contains numerous commands: "walk in a manner worthy of the calling" (Eph. 4:1); "walk in a manner worthy of the Lord" (Col. 1:10); and "walk in a manner worthy of God" (1 Thess. 2:12). It has a host of injunctions to practice specific virtues, and to put away certain evil practices, such as anger, wrath, malice, slander, and foul talk (Col. 3:8). All these Scripture passages form powerful arguments for the individual's responsibility.

Sanctification and Perfection

A major issue concerning sanctification is the question of perfection. Can we expect in this life to reach a state of total sanctification or sinless perfection, in which we never commit sin? Christians are divided in their opinions over this issue. One group, termed *perfectionists*, teaches that such perfection is possible and that each Christian should strive to reach it. John Wesley, the founder of Methodism, was said to hold such a view. Other sincere Christians, however, hold that such sinlessness will be realized only after this life.

Perfection advocates cite a number of Scripture passages to support their position. One group of passages urges believers to be perfect: "Therefore you are to be perfect, as your heavenly Father is perfect" (Matt. 5:48); "Let us go on unto perfection" (Heb. 6:1 KJV); "But let patience have her perfect work, that ye may be perfect and entire, wanting nothing" (James 1:4 KJV). The writer to the Hebrews also hinted at this: "Now the God of peace, who brought up from the dead the great Shepherd of the sheep through the blood of the eternal covenant, even Jesus our Lord, equip you in every good thing to do His will, working in us that which is pleasing in His sight, through Jesus Christ" (Heb. 13:20–21).

Other passages seem to say the Christian does not and cannot sin: "No one who abides in Him sins; no one who sins has seen Him or knows Him" (1 John 3:6). "No one who is born of God practices sin, because His seed abides in him; and he cannot sin, because he is born of God" (1 John 3:9). This combination of texts makes an impressive case for the perfectionists' position.

On the other hand, other passages imply that sinlessness is not for this life and this world. John wrote, "If we say that we have no sin, we are deceiving ourselves, and the truth is not in us. . . . If we say that we have not sinned, we make Him a liar, and His word is not in us" (1 John 1:8, 10). There is also Paul's impassioned outcry in Romans 7:15: "For that which I am doing, I do not understand; for I am not practicing what I would like to do, but I am doing the very thing I hate." In addition, none of the spiritual giants of Scripture are described as having reached perfection. On the contrary, there is plenty of evidence of sin throughout the lives of these men and women.

How, then, shall we resolve this dilemma? We may begin by noting that the statements in 1 John about sinlessness are in the perfect tense of the Greek verb. This tense indicates continuous action. We might translate these verses as follows: "No one who abides in him sins continually; no one who continually sins has either seen him or known him. . . . He who regularly practices sin is of the devil. . . . No one born of God regularly commits sin; for God's nature abides in him, and he cannot persistently sin because he is born of God." This casts a very different light on the picture. The text is not saying that a believer is delivered from ever sinning. Instead, it announces that the sinner is no longer under the constant domination of sin. That is quite a different thing.

The verses prescribing perfection also deserve examination. Actually, the word here translated "perfect" should not be translated "flawless." The meaning is "complete" or "mature." The picture of perfection can be compared to a full-grown plant—it has all the parts it is intended to have. No essential part is missing.

In this sense, my car is a perfect automobile. It is not mechanically flawless. For that matter, it wasn't perfect when it rolled off the assembly line three and one-half years and 68,000 miles ago. It is complete, however. It has an engine with six cylinders, each with its own piston, rings, wrist pin, connecting rod, and bearings attached to the crankshaft. Each has a spark plug and two valves. There are fuel injectors, a coil, a distributor, a transmission, a drive train, four wheels and tires, front and rear suspension, and steering systems.

Just so, Christians are commanded to be complete or entire. They are to have all the qualities or virtues of Christian character. They are to be fully developed and well-rounded. They are not spiritually healthy if one area is extremely developed but another is stunted. That is a spiritual deformity. Rather they are to grow up into the full measure of the stature of Christ (Eph. 4:13).

When we think of sin as merely external acts, it is possible to conceive of ourselves as sinless. But, as Jesus pointed out, sin is far more than that: it is any wrong thought, attitude, or intention as well. He taught that we will not gain God's approval because we haven't committed murder, if instead we hate our brother (Matt. 5:21–22). Nor could a man consider himself blameless for not having committed adultery with a woman, if he looked at her lustfully. In his heart he has already committed adultery with her (Matt. 5:27–28). When seen this way, can any of us say we are totally sinless?

Why should we strive for perfection, then, if it is unattainable? The fact that we will never achieve the ideal does not mean that we should not seek it. Sanctification is like a ship that uses the North Star as a navigational reference point when sailing north. There is no recorded instance of a ship ever reaching the North Star by sailing toward it. Yet it is still the standard toward which we aim.

So it is with sinlessness. The standard is undoubtedly that we should someday be completely free from every sin. Although we will never reach sinless perfection in this life, it pleases God that we follow this standard as closely as possible. And it is this which will be our destiny in the life to follow.

Study Guide

Key Questions

1. What are the two meanings of sanctification the author gives?
2. What are the differences between completeness and perfection in the spirit-filled Christian?
3. Why should we as Christians strive for spiritual perfection?

Bible Investigation

1. Look at Jesus' words in Matthew 5:48 and Matthew 5:21–22, 27–28. How do we reconcile these ideas?
2. In Matthew 6:1 Jesus says that doing acts of righteousness to be seen by others is not commendable. In fact, heart attitude is as important as a righteous act. Can you think of Bible characters who did a righteous act with the wrong attitude?
3. Read Ephesians 4:13. What does it mean to grow up into the full measure of the stature of Christ? How does this expression compare with the author's idea of completeness?

Personal Application

If sin can be wrong attitudes, thoughts, or intentions, as Jesus said, how can Christians try to eliminate such sins? Is it possible to eliminate wrong attitudes in our everyday life? How do we work at this problem?

For Further Thought

1. Is it better to have a goal of sinlessness in our daily living or to live life knowing that we are surely going to sin sometimes? How do each of these convictions change the way we live our lives?
2. A church sign recently proclaimed to its community "Where we go hereafter depends on what we go after here." How does this relate to Jesus' words in Matthew 5? How much does the process of sanctification have to do with attitude rather than deeds?

10

The Good Life

The Christian life was never intended to be a static existence. It is to be lived, enjoyed, developed. Living as Christians gives us several new resources and responsibilities.

Assurance of Salvation

The first resource is assurance of salvation. God intends that each person should not only be saved, but also know that he or she is saved. John indicated that his reason for writing his Gospel was "that you may believe that Jesus is the Christ, the Son of God, and that believing you may have life in His name" (John 20:31). His purpose in writing his first letter to believers was "that you may know that you have eternal life" (1 John 5:13).

It is possible to have salvation without being certain of it. This is not a desirable situation, because the Christian without assurance does not work effectively. Inner strength and resources are turned inward to cope with anxieties and doubts. It is possible for a genuine believer to lack assurance. We need to examine the basis of our assurance.

Lack of assurance may result from several factors. It may come from our excessive preoccupation with a certain type of emotional experience, which we may think every believer must have. Our failure to have such an experience creates uncertainty. Or we may have an abnormal concern over our lack of spiritual perfection. As we noted earlier, the experience of conversion varies greatly from one person to another. Furthermore, we should measure our progress in the Christian life by our distance from the beginning point, not our nearness to the ultimate destination. If we want certainty we can gain it only by giving our attention to what is certain. We can't concentrate on the unclear.

The first source of assurance is the Word of God. John told his readers that his message to them was not totally new, but was based on a command they already had (1 John 2:7). Today, we have the New Testament Scriptures as well. And what do those Scriptures tell us? Wherever we find genuine trust in Jesus Christ, there we have new life. "But as many as received Him, to them He gave the right to become children of God, even to those who believe in His name" (John 1:12). According to Romans 10:13, "whoever will call upon the name of the Lord will be saved." The real question then is simply, "Have you trusted in Christ's saving work, and are you doing so now?" If the answer is Yes, then God says, "You are my child." This is true regardless of our personal feelings, our health, or the weather.

The second source of assurance is the works of Christian living. In his first letter John pointed to several works. One is keeping the Lord's commandments (2:3–5). Accepting Christ is taking him as Savior and Lord, and this leads to obedience. Those who keep his commands not only do what he says but also what he does; as a result they grow in likeness to him (2:6).

Another work John mentioned is love for the brethren (2:7–11; 3:11–18). True salvation alters our affections. We not only feel drawn to the people of God, but we are genuinely concerned for their welfare and do what we can for them. Frequently, our feelings follow, rather than precede, our actions. But if we are part of one body in Christ, we will feel the hurts and happiness of other members, rejoicing with those who rejoice and weeping with those who weep.

An additional work of Christian living is keeping the doctrine of Christ. In John's day some were denying the reality of Christ's physical human nature, so the Apostle spoke out clearly against such teaching (1 John 4:1–6; 5:1). He identified as "of God" all those who believed fully in the doctrine of Christ. And so it is with us. If we really know Jesus, we will give him the full status he deserves, not whittling down in any way his exalted position as Savior and Lord.

All these works in the life of Christians are evidences that God has entered their lives and made a real difference in their personalities. These works are not a set of standards by which to evaluate the reality of other Christians' lives. They are evidences for oneself. When Jesus healed the blind man (John 9) and the lame man (Matt. 9:1–8) they experienced an immediate and obvious change in behavior. So will we. If we have been spiritually healed, it should be apparent in what we are, how we feel, and what we do, although it doesn't mean we won't sometimes fail or fall short.

The final source of assurance is the witness of the Holy Spirit. John indicated that the Spirit who has been given to us is proof that we know that we abide in him (1 John 3:24; 4:13). The Spirit works in several ways to bring about the conviction, the deep-settled certainty, that we are God's children. One means is through the sense of sonship. The Spirit, Paul said, moves us to cry out, "Abba! Father!" (Rom. 8:15; Gal. 4:6).

The Spirit also works in us, calling to mind the words of our Lord, underscoring them, giving us understanding of them, and bearing witness to Christ (John 14:25–26; 16:13–15). Sometimes he magnifies for us the grace of God, so that we see clearly that we are transformed creatures and that the most significant factor in our lives is our relationship to Christ.

The Leading of God's Spirit

A second major resource of the Christian life is the leadership of the Spirit of God. Paul wrote, "For all who are being led by the Spirit of God, these are sons of God" (Rom. 8:14). He also drew a contrast between walking by (or living by) the Spirit (Gal. 5:16, 25) and gratifying the flesh (Gal. 5:13, 16). The Christian is supposed to live under the Holy Spirit's control and seek to please Christ. On the one hand, to live this way is an obligation. On the other hand, it is a privilege to be led by God. The question is how we determine what God wants us to do. There are several sources of this guidance.

The most important is the teaching of the Bible. The Scriptures speak clearly on many broad issues of life. On these matters we need no further information. Many issues, however, are not specifically addressed. This is due in part to the fact that biblical revelation was given in a culture vastly different from our own. Even when the Bible has no specific information, however, it lays down principles for guidance, but we must be aware of them and know how to apply them to life.

The second source of guidance is the Holy Spirit's illuminating work. Jesus' teaching about the Holy Spirit applies more fully to guidance than to assurance. If we allow him, he will guide us into the truth of God's will for our lives. It is a matter of consciously giving the Holy Spirit control over our lives. Out of the confused mass of ideas, feelings, suggestions, and hopes, the Spirit creates clarity. He brings our lives into focus. Once properly adjusted, just like an image on a television screen, the torn snatches of light "lock" into a clear picture.

God also leads us through life's circumstances. Among the most obvious cases of this is the story of Gideon in Judges 6:36–40. Wanting to be certain that God would use him to deliver Israel from the Amalekites, Gideon prayed that God would first make a fleece wet while keeping the surrounding threshing floor dry. Then he asked that the fleece would be dry and the ground around it wet. In each case the Lord did precisely what Gideon asked. Gideon thus knew God was leading him. God, who is Lord of all, is able to control the course of events, and thus open certain opportunities to his followers.

Circumstances, however, are not an infallible source of divine guidance. In fact, they carry the danger of superstition. For that reason, they must always come third in priority, behind the Bible and the Holy Spirit's inward working. But circumstances are an important channel for God's direction, and when carefully used and interpreted, certain situations can be used to our advantage.

Finally, God leads through the counsel of other godly believers. Moses, for example, was unable to see the solution to his problem of overwork. His father-in-law, Jethro, observed his predicament and suggested that he delegate some of his labors to others—a bit of counsel that worked out very well (Exod. 18:13–27). Jethro, not so closely involved in what was happening and as a result more objective, could be a source for Moses' own self-understanding.

So God often uses our fellow believers to help us see his will. It isn't that our friends discover God's will for us. God reveals his will to the individual involved, not to someone else. Nonetheless, another person can suggest an idea we may never have considered and so help us see God's will for ourselves.

Participation in the Church

This brings us to the third resource and responsibility: involvement in the church. Jesus indicated that he would establish the church, and that it would play a powerful role in the continuation of his ministry (Matt. 16:13–20). The church was to consist of all believers at all times and in all places. Specifically, however, it would also mean local gatherings of believers in particular places and times. The early believers gathered, often in small groups in homes. The writer to the Hebrews urged and encouraged his readers not to neglect their meeting with each other (Heb. 10:25).

One of the benefits of participation in the church is instruction. In each local assembly in the early church there were pastor-teachers who taught the revealed Word of God. These local bodies, then, were centers of that discipling Jesus commanded in his Great Commission (Matt. 28:19–20). Today, the local church gathers for preparation before going out to serve.

The church is also a place for worship. While there is great value in individual devotional experience, God ordained the church for our collective expressions of prayer, praise, and hymn singing. Here, too, we observe the memorial Supper. Commemorating the Lord's death is to be carried out, as he commanded, until he comes again (1 Cor. 11:23–26).

In the church Christians also build up one another. On several occasions, Paul used the figure of the body to describe the church (Rom. 12:3–8; 1 Cor. 12:4–31; Eph. 1:23; 2:16; 4:4–16; Col. 1:18; 2:19; 3:15). This body has many members or organs, each of which represents an individual believer. A Christian isolated from other Christians will be a less effective, satisfied, and complete Christian, like a limb amputated from the physical body.

Because no single Christian has all the gifts needed for growth in the Christian life, each needs the others. There is no basis for one believer to feel arrogant because of what he or she has or is, or ashamed because of what he or she lacks. It is the Spirit of God who has determined in his own sovereign plan who should have which gift, and all are important (1 Cor. 12:11, 14–26).

In the church one member may have insights another lacks. Hence a "rounding effect" results from our interaction. In isolation we may develop some unusual or eccentric ideas and continue to foster them, overlooking other important aspects of Christian truth. In a group, the shortcomings of limited insights become apparent and neglected needs can be met.

Some in the body will have special gifts, others will not. Some will have the gift of teaching, which others lack. Still others will have special gifts and abilities in counseling or administration. Many other gifts will be present in the body although no one member will possess them all.

Service

The fourth responsibility is service. Jesus called his disciples *servants*. Even those in positions of leadership and authority within the group were not to be domineering, but were to serve (Mark 10:35–45).

The primary service we render in the Christian life is the propagation of the gospel message throughout the world. In his Great Commission, Jesus laid this responsibility upon his apostles (Matt. 28:19–20). The commission looked beyond the little cluster of disciples to the whole world. Today, every Christian is able to be a witness in his or her own immediate area. Beyond our own neighborhoods, however, we cannot effectively carry out the commission on our own. As a body, the church can witness within a larger radius, and establish other stations of witness in adjoining locales. Still, there is a problem with witnessing "to the end of the earth." No individual can hope to do that in a direct fashion; nor, for that matter, can a single church. But when churches unite and send their representatives to other parts of the world, they share in the work with their financial and prayer support. In this way, churches can "preach by proxy."

With financial support we can extend our service for Christ. What is a dollar bill but a symbolic equivalent of part of ourselves? Employees trade themselves for a period of time, in effect, selling a part of life to their employer. In return, the employer pays employees a sum of money. That dollar bill is, in a sense, a concentrated part of the person. When it is placed in the offering plate a part of the employee goes into that offering, and throughout the world to carry out the commission to spread the gospel.

The church is not only a place in which members are ministered to; it is also a place to minister. Minister is not restricted to an elite group of professional clergy. All Christians can minister to one another. Jesus said that this is one way we can serve him.

Sometimes Christians wish they could do something directly for the Lord. They think of men and women who were present during his lifetime and who washed his feet. They think, "If I had been at the cross, I could have offered cold water to him when he thirsted. How satisfying to be able to be of such help and mercy!" Unfortunately, this has been impossible for anyone for almost two thousand years. Yet Jesus said that there is an equivalent of such service. If it is done to "one of the least" of Jesus' brethren, it is done to him (Matt. 25:34–40).

The Christian's influence is to extend beyond the fellowship of believers. Jesus did not always require evidence of faith in him before he healed someone in need. He said that Christians are "the salt of the earth" (Matt. 5:13) and "the light of the world" (Matt. 5:14). Both individually and as the collective body of Christ, they are to minister to human needs.

Every part of the body has its own appropriate role to play. While no one has all the gifts, each member has at least one. This means that each of us should be actively engaged in using whatever ability God has given him or her. No service is too lowly; none is without significance in God's eyes.

In Jesus' parable of the talents, a servant was not rewarded for how much he did, nor for the size of the results, but for his faithfulness in using what he had been given (Matt. 25:14–30). When one is faithful in small things, he or she is given larger things to oversee.

In our service of the Lord, the Bible emphasizes Christian maturity and the effectiveness of service. Activities and possessions are usually neither "good" nor "bad." Often we are faced with several possible choices of "good." The issue then is more penetrating.

Paul used the image of a soldier to make the point (2 Tim. 2:3–4). A soldier, Paul argued, voluntarily decides not to engage in "civilian" activities. These activities may be "good" in themselves but he cannot pursue them and fulfill his assignment as a soldier. So also with the athlete (v. 5). He must compete according to the rules if he wants to win. The same is true of the hardworking farmer, who rightfully receives the first share of the crops. The Christian life, Paul argued, is a serious and important matter, and every aspect of life is evaluated in terms of its contribution to spiritual development.

Many Christians feel inadequate for the tasks they are asked to do. Anyone who has served on a church nominating committee knows how powerful this sense of inadequacy can be. Even Moses felt it when the Lord called him to lead the people of Israel out of Egypt (Exod. 3:1–4:17). He offered a whole series of excuses. In each case, however, God offered a response. He would be with Moses, enabling him to speak (4:12) and giving him evidences of his power (4:9).

In the same way, believers frequently feel the magnitude of their tasks and the limits of their own ability and strength. In reality, however, spiritual results are only partially dependent on the Christian's ability. It is the empowering Holy Spirit who takes what we do and accomplishes what no mere human effort can ever produce.

Take, for example, Peter's amazing sermon on Pentecost Sunday. Peter was not a highly trained man, nor was he gifted with oratorical abilities. Some could say the sermon, from the standpoint of the theory and practice of preaching, could be improved. But the results could scarcely be! Commenting on the sermon one pastor observed, "Peter preached the sermon, and had three thousand converts. We preach three thousand sermons, and are lucky to have one convert." Whenever we are truly seeking to serve God in what he has given us to do, we can be certain that his Spirit will be there, empowering us.

Study Guide

Key Questions

1. What are the four main resources and responsibilities of the Christian life?
2. What are the works of Christian living that are part of our assurance of salvation?

3. One resource the Christian has for living the good life is the leading of the Spirit in his or her life. What's the major source the Spirit uses in leading believers? How important, then, are sermons, group Bible studies, and personal Bible study?
4. Why is it important that circumstances of life not be used as a source for spiritual guidance apart from biblical teaching?
5. Why is Paul's picture of the human body being like the church so appropriate?

Bible Investigation

Because the Bible is a major source for Christian living, how much time should the Christian spend studying it? As you think about the entire Bible, can you think of ways we get guidance from the Old Testament narratives? the books of poetry (Psalms, Proverbs, Ecclesiastes, Song of Solomon)? the Prophets? the Book of Revelation?

Personal Application

Jesus' parable of talents (Matt. 25:14–30) points out that we are only responsible for using the gifts that have been given to us. This can be reassuring to those of us who have no gifts for singing, preaching, or evangelizing, but what does it tell us about assessing our own gifts and our using or not using them? Should this be a major concern to us? Why or why not?

11

Long-Lasting Christianity

Sometimes the Christian seems like a person clinging to the edge of a cliff, desperately hanging on by her fingernails, in danger of dropping to her destruction. Must the believer live in this insecurity, constantly fearing the loss of what is most precious to her? The teaching of the "eternal security of the believer" or of "perseverance of the saints" speaks to this question and concern.

Two Views

There are marked differences of conviction among evangelical Christians regarding a believer's security. Bible-believing Christians are divided into two major camps in their understanding of this issue. One group, often called Calvinists, after the teaching of the Reformation theologian John Calvin, maintains that genuinely regenerate persons cannot "fall away" and lose their salvation. While they may falter or backslide temporarily, they will never fully and permanently apostasize. The slogan sometimes attached to this view is "once saved, always saved."

Those who hold this view use a number of Scriptures that suggest the permanence of salvation for all who believe. One well-known New Testament passage is John 10:27–30: "My sheep hear My voice, and I know them, and they follow Me; and I give eternal life to them, and they shall never perish, and no one shall snatch them out of My hand. My Father, who has given them to Me, is greater than all, and no one is able to snatch them out of the Father's hand. I and the Father are one." This seems to be a clear statement of the permanence of saving grace. A similar emphasis appears in Romans 8:35–39. The final two verses of the passage read: "For I am convinced that neither death, nor life, nor angels, nor principalities, nor things present, nor things to come, nor powers, nor height, nor depth, nor any other created thing, shall be able to separate us from the love of God, which is in Christ Jesus our Lord." Other Scriptures frequently cited include Philippians 1:6, Romans 8:29, Romans 11:29, 2 Timothy 1:12, and 1 Peter 1:5.

In addition to these Scriptures, there is also a theological argument. In regeneration, God produces a change in the believer's soul. The person's very nature and disposition are altered. How then can one lose that salvation, since that would require the reversal of regeneration? How could such a thing happen? What would de-regeneration mean? Isn't God's work of regeneration permanent?

Sometimes in popular circles this Calvinistic position is extended to teach that Christians cannot lose their salvation no matter what they do. Thus, even though they fall into gross sin and remain in it, they are eternally secure. This, however, is a distortion of what Calvinists have generally meant by the security of the believer or the perseverance of the saints.

The other major camp, often called *Arminianism,*
believes that it is possible for a genuine Christian to fall
away from grace and lose salvation, and that indeed
some actually do. While some Arminians—named after
the sixteenth-century Dutch theologian Jacobus
Arminius—teach that it is possible to lose salvation and
regain it, others maintain that salvation, once lost, can
never be regained.

Those holding this view give several arguments. The
first and most significant is based on Scripture passages
that contain severe warnings to those who abandon their
faith. Especially prominent are the warning passages in
the Book of Hebrews. One of the most pointed is
Hebrews 6:4–6: "For in the case of those who have once
been enlightened and have tasted of the heavenly gift
and have been made partakers of the Holy Spirit, and
have tasted the good word of God and the powers of the
age to come, and then have fallen away, it is impossible
to renew them again to repentance, since they again cru-
cify to themselves the Son of God, and put Him to open
shame." Even Paul seemed concerned about the possibility of losing favor with God (some would interpret to
mean his salvation) when he wrote: "But I buffet my
body and make it my slave, lest possibly, after I have
preached to others, I myself should be disqualified"
(1 Cor. 9:27). Other Scriptures cited include Mark 13:13,
1 Corinthians 15:2, and Hebrews 10:28–29.

In addition to these passages, there are the apparent
instances of believers who lost their salvation. King Saul
is an outstanding example. Although chosen by God and
endowed with every blessing and advantage, Saul ended
his life tragically separated from God's favor. Judas Iscar-
iot, another example, was not only a follower of Jesus
but one of the chosen inner circle of Twelve who were
the Lord's special servants and confidants. Yet he
betrayed his Master and ended his own life filled with

remorse but no genuine repentance. Ananias and Sapphira (Acts 5:1–11) and Demas (Col. 4:14; 2 Tim. 4:10; Philem. 24) are other individuals cited in support of this position.

This appeal to individual cases is extended beyond the Bible. One hears of persons who made outstanding professions of faith, whose Christian lives were respected and commended by other believers, but who later totally rejected their earlier commitments. Some may even have been leaders in the Christian community. I call this the "I knew a person who . . . " argument. It is an experiential parallel to the biblical instances we noted.

Examination of Biblical Teachings

Is there any clear way to bring all these considerations together into a singular, coherent view? The logical starting point should be the key Scriptures. Let us look more closely at two of the passages cited on opposite sides of the controversy, John 10:27–30 and Hebrews 6:4–6.

John's statement is a declaration of the permanence of the salvation that the Lord gives to believers. Jesus simply stated: "My sheep hear My voice, and I know them, and they follow Me; and I give eternal life to them." Then he elaborated with a powerful statement, "and they shall never perish; and no one shall snatch them out of My hand." He concluded by declaring the greatness of the Father who keeps the sheep, and then affirming his oneness with the Father.

The key portion of the passage, however, is "they shall not perish." This claim deserves closer examination. John reported Jesus' sayings by using a double negative. While this is poor English usage, it is appropriately used in Greek to show an emphatic denial. John also used a verb tense that indicates the action is thought of as a single event; the mood is one of possibility rather than actuality. To paraphrase his statement, it is as if he is saying: "They shall not—they shall not—perish at all, by any stretch of the imagination." It is hard to imagine a more emphatic way of making the point. If taken as an all-inclusive description of Jesus' followers, this certainly denies that any ever do fall away.

The Hebrews 6 passage is more difficult, since it can be interpreted in at least three different ways:

1. That these are people who never were genuine believers. Thus their rejection of the faith is real, but it is a rejection, rather than a departure. They were exposed to the gospel and "sampled" it, but were not born again.
2. That these are genuine believers, and that they really do fall away. Thus the passage not only teaches the possibility of Christians losing their salvation, but demonstrates the actuality of it.
3. That these are genuine believers, but they do not actually abandon their faith and commitment. These are merely hypothetical cases. They are descriptions of what would happen, *if* a believer were to repudiate the decision to follow the Lord. As such, they are *warnings*, intended to help prevent such an occurrence.

The first and third interpretations fit the Calvinistic view, while the second fits well with the Arminian position. But how will we decide among them?

Whatever interpretation one adopts, this Hebrews passage does not show that it is possible to lose one's salvation and regain it. If these are genuinely regenerate persons and if they do lose their salvation, then it is clear that it is impossible to restore them again to repentance.

Second, it is difficult to deny the genuineness of these persons' salvation. The terms describing them make that quite clear: "Who have once been enlightened and have tasted of the heavenly gift and have been made partakers of the Holy Spirit" (Heb. 6:4) is especially impressive. The word "partakers" literally means "to share in" the Holy Spirit. Certainly these people must have been born again.

Third, the major issue is the meaning of one word, translated in most of the versions, "if they fall away." Actually, this is not in a standard Greek hypothetical form. Rather we have here an adverbial participle that means literally "falling away," but which may yield numerous possible translations. It may be rendered, "when they fall away," "so that they fall away," "because they fall away," "in order to fall away," and several other possibilities. One justifiable rendition is certainly, "if they fall away," but the meaning cannot be determined by the word and its form alone. The context of the phrase is also important.

The key clue to this puzzle is found in verse 9: "But, beloved, we are convinced of better things concerning you, and things that accompany salvation, though we are speaking in this way." The inspired author assumed that his readers had salvation and that they would not experience the fate described in verses 4–6. This evidence supports the third interpretation: that these are hypothetical cases, indicating what it would be like if a genuine Christian did abandon commitment to the Lord, but not affirming that any actually do so.

We now want to give a more comprehensive position regarding a believer's security, drawing together this material and some matters we mentioned earlier. It is possible for Christians to lose their salvation, but no one ever does. There is a parallel here to the temptation of Jesus. If Jesus' temptation was genuine (which we must believe, if Scripture is to be taken seriously), then it must have been *possible* for him to have sinned. Yet he *did not*, and we may even say that it was *sure* that he *would not*. Similarly, there is no real contradiction between John 10 and Hebrews 6. Hebrews 6:4–8 describes what would happen if a believer were to apostasize, without suggesting that any ever do. Indeed, verse 9 suggests that true believers do not, a teaching that is also the basic thrust of John 10.

Biblical Examples

Saul provides us with an Old Testament example of an apostate believer, which is a bit difficult to handle because the teaching concerning the Holy Spirit indwelling believers had not yet been revealed in Scripture. It therefore seems somewhat inappropriate to use Saul as a model because his anointing by the Spirit was to make him a king and was not a seal of his salvation. Saul showed some signs of spiritual weakness very early. Judas is more instructive. His denial of Christ seems clear and definite. When we seek evidence of genuine regeneration in his life, however, we are hard pressed to find any. In fact, John 12:6 indicates that his supposed faith may have been false all along. Judas became indignant over Mary anointing Jesus' feet with the costly ointment of pure nard, complaining that this ointment could have been sold and the proceeds given to the poor. John's explanation, however, is otherwise: "Now he said this, not because he was concerned about the poor, but because he was a thief, and as he had the money box, he used to pilfer what was put into it" (John 12:6).

We know relatively little about Demas. At one point Paul spoke of him as a "profitable" member of his team (Col. 4:14; Philem. 24). But it is impossible to determine the nature, extent, or permanence of his departure from the Pauline fellowship.

Indeed, there are some biblical instances of persons who were evidently genuine believers, but who failed and fell into sin. David is one of these. A "man after God's own heart" (1 Sam. 13:14), he nevertheless sinned grievously. In the process of trying to conceal his acts, one major sin led to another. As a result, his relationship with the Lord was damaged. In Psalm 51 we read his penitential outcry: "Restore to me the joy of Thy salvation" (v. 12). Nothing in the passage would indicate that David had lost his salvation, but he needed the restoration of joy. David did sincerely repent and later he was restored by God to a position of usefulness and blessing.

The same is true of Peter. Brash and self-confident Peter assured Jesus that he would never deny him. When he did, he was bitterly repentant (Luke 22:61–62). Peter, however, never abandoned faith in Christ. The last reports of his life (Acts; 1 and 2 Peter) suggest a complete restoration.

These two biblical instances seem to be the general pattern for Christians who do sin. Numerous others could be found, such as Moses, Elijah, and other members of the Twelve. Temporary sin and setback were common but always short of the loss of the salvation relationship.

We can make two important observations from these biblical instances. First, not everyone who makes a profession, even an impressive profession, is necessarily a genuine believer. Jesus pointed out that the true and the false may be found together, and at an early stage of development they may not be easily distinguishable (Matt. 13:24–30). Some who have thought of themselves as true followers and who have even performed impressive works will hear him say, "I never knew you; depart from me, you evildoers" (Matt. 7:21–23 RSV).

The "Person Who"

This points up the difficulty in using the "I knew a person who . . ." approach. We need a great deal of information to evaluate such cases. Was the original commitment genuine? What is the extent of the departure? Is the person dead yet? The Bible should be used to prove experience; experience should not be used to prove the Bible.

Furthermore, cases can always be found to support one side or the other. On one occasion, when I was a pastor in Chicago, an evangelist holding services in my church told me about an incident in a Michigan church. He was having dinner with one of the leading families of the church. The wife was a highly respected church member. Her testimony and active involvement in the Lord's work were well known. She was considered a model Christian. After the meal, as the evangelist was about to leave, she approached him and in desperation said, "Pray for me, I need to become a Christian." She had considered herself a Christian, as had everyone else. In that moment, however, she realized that she had never been truly converted.

Suppose that before reaching this point she had turned her back on the Christian faith. She would have become another instance of "I know a Christian who . . ." It seems safer to place our reliance on the Bible's teaching in these matters than on experiential instances.

We also need to distinguish between temporary abandonment of Christian commitment (backsliding) and permanent departure (apostasy). We have instances of the former in the Bible, but not of the latter. This was my point in considering Peter and David. All of us sin, and at times we may even drift into a spiritually inactive state. This, however, is scarcely the same as apostasy.

The Place of Freedom

We have purposefully avoided using the expression "perseverance of the saints." The maintenance of Christians in the faith is not primarily their doing. It is a result of God's gracious working in their lives. Thus Peter referred to "an inheritance which is imperishable and undefiled and will not fade away, reserved in heaven for you, who are protected by the power of God through faith for a salvation ready to be revealed in the last time" (1 Peter 1:4–5). We should never take credit for this—as if it were our own accomplishment. We should take courage and hope in realizing that God is guarding us, motivating us to persevere. The warnings encourage us to exercise our free will to persevere.

If I live on a busy street and I don't want my five-year-old daughter to wander into the traffic and be struck by a passing car, there are two ways I can help guarantee her safety. One is by building a high, strong fence around the yard, making it physically impossible for her to leave unassisted. This is like the false concept some have of the believer's security: a denial of any freedom, so that the believer will make no attempt to leave the faith. This is not the biblical teaching.

The other way to insure my daughter's safety is to instruct her not to go into the street, warn her of the dangers, and create a desire within her to remain in the yard. She could easily enter the street, but she would not freely choose to do it. This is how God keeps us from straying. He warns us of the dangers and gives us positive encouragement to continue and grow in the Christian faith.

There is no basis for presumption in the Christian life, but neither is there need for anxiety. Jesus indicated that although true and counterfeit believers cannot always be distinguished during this life, the true believer will endure to the end (Matt. 10:22; 24:13; Mark 13:13). Although his remarks were made about the tribulation period, they could apply to other instances as well. He prayed that the Father would keep his followers, as he had kept them so that none of them would be lost, except "the son of perdition" (John 17:11–12).

We may rejoice in this great truth, joining our testimony with Paul's: "For I know whom I have believed and I am convinced that He is able to guard what I have entrusted to Him until that day" (2 Tim. 1:12).

Study Guide

Key Questions

1. Describe John Calvin's position on eternal security regarding our salvation. What major Scripture portions did he use?
2. Describe Jacobus Arminius's position on eternal security regarding our salvation. What major Scripture portions did he use?
3. What is the author's position relative to Calvin's and Arminius's?

Bible Investigation

1. The story of Peter is a favorite of many people, although some readers may be offended by his brashness. What lessons do we learn from his life as it relates to the security of our salvation?
2. First John 3:6 makes it clear that a person who continues to sin has not known God. Which view, Arminianism or Calvinism, seems to agree most with this? How much of that question rests on the meaning of the term "know"?

Personal Application

Perhaps most of us know people who once seemed to be sincere Christians, but later lost interest completely in the Christian life. What should our attitude be toward these people? Should we remind them of the biblical passages mentioned in this chapter? pray for them? ignore them? Are these responses related to our personal view of eternal security?

For Further Thought

In both the Calvinist and Arminian view, the sheep, or believers, are admonished to follow the Shepherd, or to imitate those of faith (Heb. 6:12). Is this doctrinal question an insurmountable obstacle to the church's unity?

12

The Best Is Yet to Come

As believers, we sometimes grow weary. We seem to be so far from what we hope to be and know we ought to be. We make such slow progress in the Christian life.

Yet we also know that our life in Christ, though not yet complete, will be someday. This future perfection we call *glorification*. We hear relatively little about this doctrine in sermons or in standard theology texts. In the Bible, however, it is often mentioned. For example, when Paul listed the elements of salvation (Rom. 8:29–30), the last to appear was glorification.

The Meaning of Glory

The concept of glory is a very rich one. No single synonym for it exists. It means honor and power, splendor and radiance. It is especially associated with the events of Jesus' life. We catch a glimpse of glory in the transfiguration of Jesus. This event parallels future glorification of believers. It also anticipated Jesus' own resurrection and ascension. Peter says that "God . . . raised Him from the dead and gave Him glory" (1 Peter 1:21).

Jesus' return from the dead was the means by which he was "designated Son of God in power according to the Spirit of holiness by his resurrection from the dead" (Rom. 1:4 RSV). In a similar way Paul described the ascension of Christ as his being "taken up in glory" (1 Tim. 3:16). His ascension led to new honor for him. Acts 2:33, 5:31, Romans 8:34, Colossians 3:1, and Ephesians 1:20 speak of his elevation to the right hand of the Father, which is a biblical way of indicating the place of authority. Then, we read, the return of Christ will be in great power and glory, in contrast to his lowliness and humiliation while he was here on earth. In Matthew 16:27, Jesus said, "The Son of man is going to come in the glory of His Father, with His angels" and he gave similar descriptions of his coming in Matthew 24:30 and 25:31; Mark 8:38; 13:26; and Luke 21:27. Finally, the New Testament speaks of Jesus Christ's glory in the future (Phil. 2:9–11; 2 Tim. 4:18).

The Future Dimension of Salvation

Throughout its pages the New Testament indicates that the salvation we now possess and experience is only the beginning of God's work in us. Much more is to come. That is why this salvation is called "a promise." Paul says, "In him you also, who have heard the word of truth, the gospel of your salvation, and have believed in him, were sealed with the promised Holy Spirit, which is the guarantee of our inheritance until we acquire possession of it, to the praise of his glory" (Eph. 1:13–14 RSV). We find a similar note in references to the Old Testament believers (Heb. 11:13, 39). God's action is simply a promise of even greater things to come.

Another way of speaking of our future salvation is found in the firstfruits image. Romans 8:23 says that the believer possesses "the first fruits of the Spirit." He is the beginning and true portion of the full blessing of God yet to come. The full harvest of our redemption will be our glorification.

On at least three occasions Paul also referred to our future salvation as the "earnest" (or pledge) given to us (2 Cor. 1:22; 5:5; Eph. 1:14). God has put his seal on us and given us his Spirit in our hearts as a guarantee or "earnest"—a deposit given as evidence of the full payment to be delivered later.

Finally, the New Testament pictures our salvation as an inheritance. While an inheritance is something to which we are entitled, we do not possess it until some future time. First Peter 1:3–5 is probably the clearest example of this idea: "By his great mercy we have been born anew to a living hope through the resurrection of Jesus Christ from the dead, and to an inheritance which is imperishable, undefiled, and unfading, kept in heaven for you, who by God's power are guarded through faith for a salvation ready to be revealed in the last time" (RSV).

Final Vindication of Believers

What specifically will this glorification mean? It means, first, the believer is spiritually perfected. One dimension of this perfection is the final realization of justification, the public vindication of our status as Christians. To be sure, we are forgiven, and justified in the moment of our conversion. We know, however, that the final great judgment will reveal publicly those whose trust is in Jesus Christ. We are now justified, but in that future event we will be *saved* in this special sense. Having been reconciled by Christ's death, we shall also be saved by his life. What Christ did in his death, he is now completing by his continuing intercessory ministry (Rom. 5:9–11). And what God has done at our initial justification, he will confirm in that final judgment. He will make a public disclosure of the justification and forgiveness of those who are trusting in him. The pictures of this last judgment given us by Jesus suggest that there will be some surprises for those who are there (Matt. 25:31–46; Luke 13:22–30).

This final vindication will overturn all the human charges brought against the believer. In Romans 8 Paul poses the question, "Who shall bring charge against God's elect?" The only one who can do so is God who justifies (v. 33). "Who is the one who condemns?" Only Christ Jesus, who died for us, was raised, and is now at the right hand of God, interceding for us (v. 34). Certainly he will not condemn. Nothing, then, can separate us from God's love in Christ (vv. 35–39). While others may bring false charges against us now, they will be unable to do so in the final judgment.

Any judgment implied by circumstances will also be nullified. The Psalmist expressed this complaint most eloquently in Psalm 73. He had been envious of the wicked, and as a result he had almost stumbled (vv. 2–3). They prospered in material things (v. 12). They seemed to escape suffering and trouble (vv. 4–5). They gave no thanks; they did not acknowledge God in their good fortune; on the contrary, they were proud and blasphemous (v. 9). The Psalmist observed this and noted that whereas he had been pure and righteous, he had found misfortune in his life (vv. 13–14).

This is often true today. Christians may struggle on in bare subsistence, while members of the crime syndicate live in mansions and travel in chauffeur-driven luxury cars. Christians sometimes suffer the tragedy of serious illness or loss of a close loved one, while godless persons all around go complacently on in their apparent good fortune. The believer may wonder whether being a Christian is really worthwhile. Sometimes the Christian faces taunts like those Jesus encountered during his temptation (Matt. 4:3, 6) and at his crucifixion (Matt. 27:39–44). Such charges, however, will not stand in the final judgment. Then justice will be administered, openly and completely. Like the rich man and Lazarus (Luke 16:25), many people will find that judgment a reversal of earthly existence.

Spiritual Perfection of Believers

Glorification also means the perfecting of the believer's moral and spiritual character. Growth in Christ-likeness, begun in regeneration and continued in sanctification, will be completed in glorification. We see this truth explained in the adjectives the Bible uses to describe the Christian's future flawlessness.

One of these is "unblemished." The term is the opposite of a word meaning "fault or cause for blame." It can also refer to a spot or blemish in a sacrificial animal. By contrast, Jesus was described as an unblemished Sacrifice (Heb. 9:14). This is how we ultimately will be when we appear before God, and this is the end purpose of Christ's redemptive work: "he has now reconciled [you] in his body of flesh by his death, in order to present you holy and blameless and irreproachable before him" (Col. 1:22 RSV).

When we appear in the presence of God, we will be so purified that there will be no imperfection in us. God's holiness will be ours. This is necessary because the unholy cannot enter the presence of him who is morally perfect, in whom there is no darkness or evil *whatsoever* (1 John 1:5). The unclean must be banished forever from the presence of this Most Holy One (Rev. 21:27; 22:15).

This future spiritual perfection includes freedom from sin. Although the new birth frees us from the enslavement and power of sin, our lives are still to a measure under the effects of sin. John pointed out to Christians that the belief that we do not sin at all is a self-deception (1 John 1:8, 10). As long as we are alive in this world, we are exposed to the ravages of temptation and thus are susceptible to sin. In the future, however, endowed with true holiness and unblemished character, we will be freed from the temptation of sin. Of course, this truth was not intended to make us comfortable in sin, but to help us understand when we do fail.

We will also be free from offensiveness or any basis for stumbling. Paul prayed in Philippians 1:10 that believers might "be pure and blameless for the day of Christ" (RSV). Thus, there will be nothing worthy of blame or censure.

Perfect Unity of Believers

God is concerned for the perfect unity among Christians. Paul urged the Ephesians to "maintain the unity of the Spirit in the bond of peace" (Eph. 4:3 RSV), for there is *one* body, Spirit, hope, Lord, faith, baptism, God and Father of all. Yet the church today contains obvious diversity. There are many denominations, each with its own doctrines, loyalties, and emphases. Within a given denomination, and even within a given local church, differences sometimes erupt into bitter debates. Some have tried to bring unity through ecumenism, involving either cooperative efforts of separate denominations in councils of churches or mergers of groups into a single denomination. The ecumenical movement, however, seems to have lost its momentum. Other Christians emphasize a spiritual oneness, an agreement or "meeting of the minds." The prayer of Jesus for his disciples was "that they may be one even as we are one, I in them and thou in me, that they may become perfectly one" (John 17:22–23 RSV). This, he said, would demonstrate to the world the reality of Christ's coming (vv. 21,

23). That unity will be complete someday. If Christ is the center of a circle and individual Christians are points on the circumference, then as those points converge on the center, they converge on one another as well.

Fullness of Knowledge

Paul sharply contrasted our present imperfect knowledge with that perfect understanding which is to come. When the perfect comes, the imperfect will pass away (1 Cor. 13:9–10). He described our present knowledge as looking into a dim mirror. Someday the seeing will be direct, face to face (v. 12). Now the knowledge is partial or fragmentary; then it will be complete understanding. It will be similar to the way the Christian is understood by God (v. 12).

This fuller knowledge relates to seeing the Lord as he really is, and thus being like him. John wrote: "Beloved, we are God's children now; it does not yet appear what we shall be, but we know that when He appears we shall be like Him, for we shall see Him as He is" (1 John 3:2 RSV). To see him fully, to know him as he really is, is an exciting prospect. For the Christian who has puzzled over portions of God's Word, yearning to understand it fully, there will be a gratifying fulfillment of his quest for knowledge.

Death and Resurrection

The glorification of the believer is linked with death and passage from this world into the presence of God. The glories and benefits of life in this world, on the one hand, and the sufferings and miseries of this life, on the other, are not worth comparing with the presence of the Lord (2 Cor. 4:17). That is why Paul wished to be absent from the body, where we walk by faith, and present with

The Best Is Yet to Come   145

the Lord, where we will have true sight (2 Cor. 5:7; Phil. 1:23). That direct communion begins with the second coming of Christ and the glorification of the body.

To understand the meaning of the resurrection of the body we must take a close look at the Bible's view of humanity. Unlike some ancient philosophies, the Bible does not picture a human as a soul imprisoned in a body. Such views usually held that the soul was good and the body was evil. Thus the soul must struggle to overcome the evil influences of the body and hopefully to escape from it entirely. In the Bible, however, a human person is both soul and body. The body is not particularly the center of sin; the soul does not need to escape. The biblical contrast is between the present corruptible bodies and the glorified bodies we shall one day have. Paul pointed out that these bodies of ours are to be made like the Lord's body: "But our commonwealth is in heaven, and from it we await a Savior, the Lord Jesus Christ, who will change our lowly body to be like his glorious body, by the power which enables him even to subject all things to himself" (Phil. 3:20–21 RSV).

In another passage Paul emphasized the contrast between corruptible and incorruptible bodies. All of us are aware that our bodies deteriorate. Physically, we reach the peak of our strength at about age twenty-two. After that we gradually begin to find that we cannot perform quite as much work as we formerly did. We tire more easily. We become more susceptible to illness. Somewhere in our forties we may need eyeglasses for reading. Hearing aids, false teeth, perhaps even hairpieces are reminders that old age is coming on. We develop aches and pains, including arthritis. We find that we learn new things with greater difficulty than before, and that things slip from our short-term memories. Eventually, the body completely ceases to function and we die.

Paul said this will change with the resurrection. The mortal or perishable body will be replaced by an immortal or undying body (1 Cor. 15:52–54). Death, or dying by degrees will no longer be possible. Paul did not describe the nature of this body in detail. Apparently it is not the same body as is buried. There is a point of contact and continuity with that body, but there is also a metamorphosis. It is, in Paul's imagery, like the seed that is sown and the new plant that arises from it (vv. 36–37).

Paul gives a series of contrasts between the body that is sown and the body that is raised:

Sown	Raised
perishable	imperishable
dishonor	honor
weakness	power
physical	spiritual

It appears that Christ's body was glorified in two stages, the resurrection and the ascension. In our case, those two steps will be joined as one, so that our new bodies will be similar to Christ's following his ascension.

Another pertinent passage is 2 Corinthians 5:1–5. Here the transience of this body is contrasted with the permanence of the future body. This is apparent even in the terms used: "the earthly tent which is our house," and "a building from God." Sensing the temporary nature of this body and desiring something better and more adequate than what we now experience, "we groan, longing to be clothed with our dwelling from heaven" (v. 2). This desire is not so much to be free from the present body as it is to have it replaced by a better one: "For while we are still in this tent, we sigh with anxiety; not that we would be unclothed, but that we would be further clothed, so that what is mortal may be swallowed up by life" (2 Cor. 5:4 RSV).

Renewal of the Creation

The Bible gives us indications that not only the human race, but also the creation, was affected by Adam's sin. Since humans were to be the ruler with dominion over the rest of creation, their fall had serious results for that creation as well. God pronounced a curse following the fall. Two areas were mentioned: (1) women were to experience anguish in childbirth (Gen. 3:16); and (2) the ground was cursed, and henceforth would bring forth thorns and thistles (vv. 17–18). Within the Garden of Eden, harmony prevailed between man and himself, man and his mate, and man and the world about him. Now all those harmonies were upset. The final reversal of the effects of sin in the last days is the transformation of the whole world order. The creation is groaning in travail together, awaiting its deliverance (Rom. 8:22).

Several New Testament passages deal with this theme. Matthew 19:28 speaks of the "new world," literally, the *regeneration*. This is probably in anticipation of the new heaven and the new earth spoken of in Revelation 21:1. This comes as a result of the passing away of the first heaven and earth, and involves the appearance of the new Jerusalem. Second Peter 3:1–13 speaks of the destruction of the old heavens and earth and the coming of the new. Romans 8:21 indicates that this enslaved creation will, like us, "be set free from its bondage to decay and obtain the glorious liberty of the children of God" (RSV).

The result is this: just as the fallen creation now contains many forces and factors causing us grief and pain, the transformation of the cosmos will remove these negative influences and make it a positive place to inhabit. Thus, John described the conditions of the new heaven and new earth: "He [God] will wipe away every tear from their eyes, and death shall be no more, neither shall there be mourning nor crying nor pain any more, for the former things have passed away" (Rev. 21:4 RSV).

Reigning with Christ

Jesus told his disciples that when he sat on his glorious throne in the new world, they who had followed him would sit on twelve thrones, judging the twelve tribes of Israel (Matt. 19:28). In 2 Timothy 2:12 Paul extended this: those who have identified with Jesus, dying, living, and enduring with him, will also reign with him. This is God's plan for participation in his glory.

We will never become divine; we will always remain human. But one day we will be morally and spiritually without blemish, as he is. Our bodies will be transformed to become like that of the ascended Christ. We will live in a transformed environment. And we will share in the power and honor of his reign. What a glorious prospect!

> Dear Saviour! when before thy bar
> All tribes and tongues assembled are,
> Among thy chosen will I be,
> At thy right hand, complete in Thee,
> Yea, justified! O blessed thought!
> And sanctified! Salvation wrought!
> Thy blood hath pardon bought for me,
> And glorified, I too shall be!
> —from the hymn "Complete in Thee" by
> A. R. Wolfe

Study Guide

Key Questions

1. Discuss the many uses of "glory" in Jesus' life.
2. What four ways does the author say that Scripture depicts our future glory?

The Best Is Yet to Come 149

3. List seven more things that Scripture promises us in our glorification.

Bible Investigation

1. First John 3:2–3 tells us that we shall be like Jesus for we shall see him as he is. What do you think being "like him" entails? Why do you think our seeing him will cause us to become like him?
2. In John 14:9 Jesus tells us that anyone who has seen him has seen the Father. Is this related to the "seeing" in 1 John 3:2–3?

Personal Application

Do you think about the time when we're in glory and we'll see our loved ones who've gone on before us? There'll be no more tears in heaven and we'll all get along because we're transformed (Phil. 3:20–21). Can anything more be added to make heaven a more perfect place?

For Further Thought

First Corinthians 13:12 says we shall know as we are known. Think how wonderful it will be to see our loved ones who've gone on to heaven before us.

Teaching Suggestions

Chapter 1. Who Am I?

Bring a baby picture to class, or several pictures from magazine ads, or a combination of both. Make a list of reasons babies are so lovable. Make another list of ways that babies are a lot of work. List ways each of these lists compares to newborn Christians (e.g., a new Christian's testimony is heartwarming like a baby's smile, etc.).

List ways being born again answers the questions of Who am I? How do I relate to the God who created me? What is expected of me because of this relationship? Add other questions as time allows, such as, What is the nature of God? What is humankind's true nature? How can these two natures come together in a parent–child relationship? What future does humankind have after death because of this relationship?

To conclude, find a newspaper or magazine feature article about Christians and Christianity. What is the message of the Christian community to the world in this article? (for example, the message might be that the Christian right is a power to be reckoned with in the present political situation).

Chapter 2. An About-Face

On the board write "Apostle Paul" and "Charles Colson." List the activities of each person before and after conversion. Add a third and/or fourth name, if you like—perhaps someone from the congregation or a historical character such as St. Augustine or Martin Luther.

Discuss the meaning of the word "conversion" and how being created in the image of God consequently means we need to know God and live in a relationship with him. Show how this relationship is possible only after humankind has had an experience of turning away from the sinful nature, and a positive experience of faith in Jesus' redemptive work on humanity's behalf. Use the list of characters on the board to exemplify this truth.

List on the board the barriers to conversion as the author discusses them. Add other barriers to the list as class members suggest them.

Ask class members to share conversion experiences. You may want to check with individuals beforehand so you are sure to get both types of experiences.

Ask the class what the author means by saying that there is one Conversion, but possibly many conversions. Close with the reminder that everyone is given the invitation to conversion, and that Jesus' parables of the lost sheep, the lost coin, and the lost son in Luke 15 show us how important this message is.

Chapter 3. I'm Truly Sorry

Write on the board the famous line from *Love Story*, "Love means never having to say you're sorry." Ask for responses of agreement and/or disagreement with this thought as it relates to the Christian life. Discuss how the Christian's redemption is based on saying and meaning "I'm sorry."

Discuss the onomatopoeic meaning of the word "repentance." You may want to give examples of onomatopoeic words, such as drip, drop, splash, ping, pong. Note how often Old and New Testament messages repeat the need for repentance.

List the three factors of true repentance on the board. Under each list write supporting Scripture references. Include Bible characters' names where appropriate. Go back to the board and number 1, 2, 3, in the order the author discusses them, and ask if the order is important and why.

How important is the step of "resolving to change"? Write CHANGE on the board, and ask the class to list some of the ways a new Christian's life should change as a result of conversion. You may want to add the categories of attitudes and actions as subheadings under CHANGE.

Look again at Luke 3:7–18. List what things are suggested for the converted listeners of John the Baptist's preaching on repentance. Discuss how John's suggestions would be fulfilled in today's church (e.g., food shelves and clothing stores for needy, etc.). What was John getting at when he told the soldiers not to extort money . . . and to be content with their pay (v. 14)?

Close with Luke 3:8.

Chapter 4. Believing Is Seeing

Write on the board the opening quotes from this chapter, one underneath the other. Draw a short arrow to the right of each quote, and ask how the Christian would change these quotes. Discuss how "faith" and "belief" in these two quotes are related. Give examples of the meanings from John 1:12, John 3:16, and Ephesians 2:8–9.

Pass out half sheets of paper to class members. Ask each to draw a cartoon or stick-figure picture of a person's relationship to both repentance and faith. Encourage creativity. Ask for volunteers to share their drawings or to redraw them on the board for the rest of the class to see.

See if there are similarities among pictures. Emphasize that repentance is a response to God's holiness and our sinfulness, and that faith is the acceptance of Jesus' gift to us of his sacrifice for our sin.

List on the board the five elements involved in faith. Under each, write key words from Scripture to help listeners connect heading with meaning. For example, under "Faith as Belief" write Peter's words from Matthew 16:16. Continue on with "Faith as Trust," "Faith and Understanding," "Faith and Doubt," and "Faith and Works."

In conclusion, have a volunteer read the final paragraph of the chapter.

Teaching Suggestions   153

Chapter 5. Out of Debt

Draw on the board an old-fashioned balance scale. Mark above one side "Good deeds" and above the other "Bad deeds." Have the class discuss, either in small groups or together, the following questions: How prevalent is the thinking that God keeps weights and balances for every person and that this is the basis of our salvation? What are the problems with this view? Ask the group(s) how the Christian's weights and balances should look in comparison to the non-Christian's.

Compare how a new Christian's weights and balances might look compared to a mature Christian's, who has walked the Christian path for many years. Ask if there is any benefit to thinking about life as a balance of good deeds and bad deeds. Answers may be widely varied, but it should be helpful to the group to note that conversion means many more good deeds than bad deeds compared to the preconverted state.

Write three columns on the board, headed by Ephesians 2:8–9; Galatians 2:16; and Mark 10:17–22. Summarize the message of each of these sets of verses. Then ask why you think Jesus responded as he did in Mark. Perhaps Jesus was simply showing that the rich young man couldn't possibly have kept all the Law if he was still so attached to his wealth. If the young man had given away all his wealth at Jesus' direction, what would that indicate about the young man? What kinds of things might Jesus be asking us to give up today before we follow him?

Discuss the three-person solution to the puzzle of each human's justification. How does each person of the three-person solution do his or her part? If this is the greatest gift of all to us, what should our response be? Ask the class to list specific things that would be appropriate.

Chapter 6. Starting Life over Again

Put the words of this old chorus on the board:

Do you know that you've been born again?
(repeat)
Does the Spirit dwell within
Bearing witness that you've been

Cleansed from every sin and stain?
Are you ready if the Lord should come
Or today your soul should claim?
Can you face eternal years
Free from doubt and dread and fears?
Do you know, beyond a shadow of a doubt,
Know that you've been born again?

Ask the class what blessings listed here are inward proof to the believer that he or she is born again. How important is it that a person be guilt-free? How does guilt imperil living life to the fullest? On the board write Spirit's indwelling as number one. Ask the class for other indications of new birth in a believer. These should include assurance of eternal life, exhibition of the fruits of the Spirit, and so on.

List on the board as many different descriptions of the pre-salvation condition of a person as possible. Then discuss Jesus' words in Matthew 19:23–26 to emphasize our inability to do anything about our condition.

Finally, list on the board all the times the New Testament speaks of regeneration, born of God, born anew, and so on, using the author's examples.

Discuss #3 under Key Questions. How does new birth or rebirth speak to the four contemporary issues listed here?

An appropriate closure would be the singing together of the chorus from the opening of the class or hearing someone sing it.

Chapter 7. Christ and the Christian, Incorporated

If available, bring to class a portion of a grapevine with some branches and grape clusters to focus thinking on John 15:5–6. If not available, bring in three candles similar to those used in the unity candle lighting services in weddings. Use the author's discussion of such candle-lighting services. Continue with a discussion of what union with Christ does not mean.

Use Key Question #1 to clarify what it means to have union in Christ and the relevance of this to Christians today. Explain that while what "union in Christ" means is difficult to explain, we know the experiences that result from this union.

Ask class members to share experiences of dying to sin and rising up to a new life, either as a baptismal experience or in some other way. This might include the way a person has changed in response to difficulties in life such as a demanding boss, an uncooperative child or co-worker, and so on.

Chapter 8. You're in the Family Now

Bring a birth certificate to class, in addition to an album of pictures of a brand-new baby, or find pictures in magazines of newborns with mother, father, and/or extended families. A family picture would also draw attention to what it means to become a member of a family. Ask class members for pictures or stories about special welcomes for adopted babies.

Form small groups. Ask each group to discuss the relationship between the two topics of adoption and forgiveness, adoption and reconciliation, and so forth, as the text discusses each. Have the leader of each group refer to the text and give a list of Scripture verses used by the author for each topic. You may want to have these topics and scriptures written out for each group to discuss. Group leaders can then share with the larger group the findings on each topic.

For closure, ask class members to think about their own birth certificates and the families into which they were born. Then ask them to think of their new birth and what that adoption meant, and to look around at their new family. Perhaps a church directory would be a tangible reminder of the local family of God. Broaden the outlook to believers in other places and countries, as well as those who have died.

Chapter 9. There's a New You Coming

In large print, write Matthew 5:48. Ask class members to read aloud Matthew 5:11–12, 21–22, 27–28, and 43–45. Pose this question: "Is it possible to reach perfection as Jesus admonishes us, with the high standards that are presented to us?"

Answer Key Question #1. List ways we become sanctified (Eph. 3:20; 5:26; 1 Thess. 5:23; Titus 2:14; Heb. 13:20–21).

Discuss the two meanings of the Greek word for form (conform) as used in Romans 8:29. In conforming, we are actually taking on the character of Jesus. Note that trials and suffering are sometimes part of conforming (Rom. 8:29; 1 Peter 1:6–7).

Ask a volunteer to read Ephesians 5:16–25. Ask the class what keeping in step with the Spirit means. Note the antithesis of living by the Spirit is living in our sinful nature.

Close with silent prayers of thanksgiving for the Spirit's ministry within each believer.

Chapter 10. The Good Life

Read the opening paragraph of this chapter aloud to the class, or write it on the board. Ask why the author says living as Christians gives us several new resources and responsibilities. Ask if this is the bad news after the Good News of salvation, or if this is also good news.

Answer Key Question #1 as a large group. Write four resources and responsibilities on the board. Then using smaller groups, designate one of these categories for each group. Ask the group leaders to take notes for their groups and report back to the larger group a summary of the findings. Ask each group to consider how each one of these categories is both a resource and responsibility: (1) assurance of salvation, (2) witness of the Holy Spirit, (3) participation in church, (4) service to others. Also discuss if and how each of the above is done more effectively by a group of believers than alone. Share findings.

Remind the class that this list of resources and responsibilities for the Christian gives individuals and churches plenty of goals or life-tasks. Remind them also that people with goals for living live happier lives, according to psychologists.

Chapter 11. Long-Lasting Christianity

"Once saved, always saved."

"God's a loving, forgiving God. He'll forgive me and understand. . . ."

Write these two statements on the board and ask the class for responses. Either in small groups or together, discuss

Arminius's view and Calvin's view of eternal security with Scripture background for each view. If using groups, make sure each leader has a copy of the essentials of the person's views and the scriptures on which they are based, either from the text or written out in brief form. Ask for each group's findings after a short period of time, and then present the author's moderating view. If class members enjoy debate, two individuals could take sides and give a two- to three-minute presentation for each point of view. Be cautious so the debate doesn't escalate into argument.

Discuss how it is possible for members of the same church to hold differing views on this issue. Clarify that this doctrine is not considered fundamental or essential for a person to be considered a true believer. You may want to review the term "fundamentalism" and/or "fundamentalist" from a church historical perspective.

Chapter 12. The Best Is Yet to Come

Write the word "heaven" on the board. Give class members a sheet of paper as they come into class. As class begins, ask each person to list what things he or she is anticipating about heaven. After a few minutes, have each person read his or her list.

Ask the class to look at their lists again and see if they can prioritize, #1 being the best. Share the top listings of persons who care to share, and add Scripture portions that promise these things.

Go over the author's headings and supporting scriptures to add to the list you already have.

For closure, read the first six lines of "The Meaning of Glory." Challenge class members to think about someone with whom they can share the blessings believers will have in heaven for all eternity. Sing together verses of "Complete in Thee."

Suggestions for Additional Readings

Chafer, Lewis Sperry. *Salvation.* Grand Rapids: Kregel, 1991.

Dominy, Bert. *God's Work of Salvation.* Nashville: Broadman, 1986.

Graham, Billy. *How to Be Born Again.* Waco, Tex.: Word, 1977.

Hull, William E. *The Christian Experience of Salvation.* Nashville: Broadman, 1987.

MacArthur, John. *The Gospel According to Jesus.* Grand Rapids: Zondervan, 1994.

Ryrie, Charles C. *So Great Salvation.* Wheaton, Ill.: Victor, 1989.

Strombeck, J. F. *So Great Salvation.* Grand Rapids: Kregel, 1992.

Warfield, Benjamin B. *The Plan of Salvation.* Grand Rapids: Eerdmans, 1942.

Warren, Virgil. *What the Bible Says about Salvation.* Joplin, Mo.: College, 1986.